Sowing in the Sunshine,
Sowing in the Shadows

Map of Ivory Coast (Cote d'Ivoire)
(with cities mentioned in this book)

Korhogo ●   •Ferkessedougou

•Katiola

Beomi•   ● Bouake

• Bocanda

Tiebissou•

Yamoussoukro●

Dimbokro•   •Toumodi

Abidjan ●

Sowing in the Sunshine, Sowing in the Shadows

BY BRENDA RITCHEY

CreateSpace
Charleston, South Carolina

Sowing in the Sunshine, Sowing in the Shadows

ISBN-13: 978-1489532800

Printed in the United States of America
CreateSpace, Charleston, South Carolina

190 Cherokee Blvd.
Toccoa, GA 30577
707-886-1684

Dedicated in memory of

Joseph Clyde Ritchey, Sr. and
Esther Samantha Stombaugh Ritchey

and

Harold Herbert Hoover and
Ethel Blanche Luke Hoover

parents of
Joseph Clyde Ritchey, Jr. and
Doris Virginia Hoover Ritchey

BRINGING IN THE SHEAVES

Knowles Shaw/George A. Minor
Public Domain

Sowing in the morning, sowing seeds of kindness,
Sowing in the noontide and the dewy eve;
Waiting for the harvest, and the time of reaping,
We shall come rejoicing, bringing in the sheaves.

Refrain:
Bringing in the sheaves, bringing in the sheaves,
We shall come rejoicing, bringing in the sheaves.
Bringing in the sheaves, bringing in the sheaves,
We shall come rejoicing, bringing in the sheaves.

Sowing in the sunshine, sowing in the shadows,
Fearing neither clouds nor winter's chilling breeze;
By and by the harvest, and the labor ended,
We shall come rejoicing, bringing in the sheaves.

Going forth with weeping, sowing for the Master,
Though the loss sustained our spirit often grieves;
When our weeping's over, He will bid us welcome,
We shall come rejoicing, bringing in the sheaves.

PART 1
THE RITCHEYS

PART 2
A HISTORY OF C&MA MISSIONS
IN IVORY COAST, WEST AFRICA

PART 1

THERE IS ALWAYS A BEGINNING!

(Note: In these first few chapters, Dad is referred to as "Bud," his family's nickname for him, since his father had the same name.)

My father Joseph Clyde Ritchey, Jr., or "Bud," as he was called by his family, was born on November 30, 1927, at home in Portage, Pennsylvania. He was the fourth of nine children, oldest of two sons. His parents were Joseph Clyde Ritchey, Sr., born September 28, 1892, and Esther Samantha Stombaugh Ritchey, born March 6, 1897.

Most of Bud's ancestors had come to America in the early 1700s, and had settled in the beautiful mountains of Blue Knob in western Pennsylvania, where they farmed the land and raised large families. They were of hearty European stock, a strong mixture of Dutch, German, English, Swiss, and Austrian. Blue Knob is Pennsylvania's second highest mountain, and is touted as "Pennsylvania's highest skiable mountain," located in Bedford County, between Johnstown and Altoona.

Bud's grandparents, John Calvin Ritchey (also

known as John Newton, since there was another John Calvin in Blue Knob) and Sarah (Sallie) Long Ritchey had nine children. Their fourth child, my grandfather, was named Joseph Clyde Ritchey, known by his middle name, Clyde. Clyde's mother Sallie described Clyde as "bullheaded." Sallie told one of her granddaughters of an occasion when the family was all dressed up and in the wagon heading for a wedding. Clyde hauled off and punched his older sister Esther in the stomach for no reason, and made her cry. Their mother Sallie stopped the wagon, pulled Clyde from the wagon, and gave him a switching. He just laughed. The more he laughed the more she switched. Finally she really gave it to him, and he started to cry. He looked up at his mother and said, "Sure! You'd rather see me bawlin' than laughin', wouldn't you?" That was too much, and Sallie started laughing. They were soon on their way again.

At the age of 23, Clyde joined the U.S. Cavalry and served from 1915 to 1919 in Brownsville, Texas during the Mexican Punitive Expedition, and later patrolled the Panama Canal.

One of Clyde's daughters recalls a time when her dad complained of a sore in his mouth. He went to see the dentist, who found something imbedded in his gums that had caused the infection. The dentist removed a piece of wood a little longer than a splinter. Clyde brought it home to show his family and then explained that while he was in the Cavalry, many years before, they had to do a lot of bayonet practice while riding their horses. He remembered a day when he ran into a branch of the tree on which the target was placed. Apparently a piece of the wood went into his gum and broke off. The cut healed and had caused him no problem for years until then.

An elderly gentleman who had lived in Brownsville as a boy during those years recalled how he would watch the Cavalry wagons roll past his house, with a chain attached to a wagon wheel to churn ice cream as they went along. Evidently there were some perks to being on the move!

Clyde, who was not a Christian at the time, nevertheless lived a fairly upright life while in the Army. He did not drink or gamble. However, he did lend money to the other men, which they would return with interest. As a result, he had quite a bankroll when he returned home. When he left the Cavalry he was a First Sergeant.

Upon his arrival back home, Clyde roomed with his sister Esther in Portage and worked at the Sonman Mine, a coalmine that had opened in 1874. Portage was located about eight miles from home in Blue Knob, and was on the 36-mile long Allegheny Portage Railroad route that included a 1,400-foot rise in elevation from the east and nearly 1,200 feet from the west. This "portage" was necessary to connect Philadelphia and Pittsburgh for commercial purposes in the mid-1800s.

Esther's husband suffered from poor health. Disturbed by his sister's difficult situation at home, Clyde asked, "Esther, how can your brothers see you like this and not do anything to help?" He handed her a large sum of money and advised her to begin a rooming house. By taking in boarders she was able to support her family and later help her daughters get the education they needed to become teachers.

Although he was not much of a churchgoer at the time, Clyde went with his sister once to hear a missionary speak. When the offering plate was passed, his sister noticed her brother placed a $10 bill in the plate—a generous amount at the time. Although Clyde had not yet given his heart to the Lord, he was already demonstrating tenderness toward the Lord's work. Much later in life he would confide to one of his daughters that if he could do it all over again, he would not have gotten married, but would have gone to serve the Lord on the mission field. Not that he regretted marrying Esther and raising a family. Not by any means! He loved his wife and family dearly. But his heart was touched by those going into eternity without knowing Christ.

Clyde's wife Esther, the second of 13 children, was also reared on a farm. Esther's younger sister Grace told about what wonderful Christian parents they had. Each night before going to bed, the family would read from the Scriptures, Dad Stombaugh would pray, then his wife prayed, followed by the family reciting the Lord's Prayer.

When asked about how she had become a Chris-

tian, Esther told of walking through a church cemetery as a young girl when she heard singing and
thought it was angels' voices. It was probably just the
church choir, but she was so moved by the beauty of
it that she fell on her knees right where she was and
asked Jesus Christ to be her Savior.

Dad Stombaugh owned his own sawmill and sur-
veyed timber for farmers. When the oldest
Stombaugh child was born, Mom Stombaugh had
gone blind for a while. This was in 1895, and the doctor advised her that if having one child would cause
temporary blindness, she had better have no more
children—who knew what would happen? Maybe
she would even die! But that didn't stop Myrtle
Stombaugh! She went on to have 12 more children.
When her next to the youngest child was a baby, she
was canning green beans on the kitchen stove when
the faulty flue caught fire and the house burned to
the ground. The large family was parceled out to relatives until a new house could be built.

The Stombaugh family loved music. They would
gather around the organ and sing hymns, accompanied by the boys on violins and guitars. This love of
music was to serve Esther well when it was her time
to leave home. As each of the Stombaugh children
reached their mid-teens, he or she was expected to
leave home and find a job to support themselves,
sending what they could spare to help support the
large family back home.

When Esther was sixteen she left home to work

for a family in Portage, helping with the housework and caring for the children. Her employers owned the brand new movie theater in Portage, the Rivoli. When it was discovered that Esther knew how to play the piano, she was hired to play the background music for the old black and white silent movies. She had a sense of humor and enjoyed teasing the audience by playing songs such as the rollicking "Roll Out the Barrel" very slowly for a sad scene, or jazzing up an old hymn for exciting scenes. People rarely noticed what was being played as they became caught up in the drama and novelty of the "silver screen."

It was during this time that Esther and Clyde met. She and Clyde began to go out on double dates with her younger sister Pearl and her beau Alvin Gordon. By this time Pearl was also working for the Bairds, Esther's employers. The young people drove around the countryside in Alvin's car, laughing and enjoying each other's company. There was no air conditioning in the car (nor anywhere else in those days), and when it rained, they had to stop to hang up the green curtains in the windows to keep from getting wet. Often by the time the curtains were hung, the rain had stopped. They also had to frequently stop to repair tires at the side of the road due to the rough road conditions, caused as well by the poor quality of the tires of the day. But they were young and in love, and these little inconveniences only added to their entertainment and sense of adventure.

After nearly two years of courting, on August 16,

1922, Esther and Clyde were married in a double ceremony with her sister Pearl and Alvin. Esther was 25 and Clyde was 30. For the two couples, the events surrounding their wedding and honeymoon were a source of hilarity for years to come. The two couples eloped to a nearby town, with only their parents and employers knowing of their plans.

When they arrived unannounced at the parsonage around 10:00 in the morning, they found the minister still in his pajamas. He excused himself to go back upstairs and get dressed. Hearing a small sound, they looked around furtively, and discovered the cook hiding under the kitchen table so as to better see what was going on, evidently hoping for obscurity. It was quite comical, and the young people had difficulty containing their laughter at such a solemn moment.

Their wedding trip was to Winchester, Virginia, where Clyde had spent some time and had many friends. They had three flat tires along the way because the roads were so bad, and they had to stop several times to hang the curtains because of rain.

When they finally got to Virginia, they found it hot and humid. The only relief from the August heat was from the electric fans in their rooms. The next day was Sunday, so they decided to attend church. The congregation was singing a hymn as the couples walked into a nearby church. They seated themselves, and when the song was completed, the pastor looked back at them and said, "I see we have strangers and visitors in our church this morning.

We're glad to have you, but you know, we go to church very early. We are just finishing our church service, but there is another church about a block and a half from here. Maybe you can get in there." The two couples were on their way again, and when they arrived at the next church, the pastor was praying. They quietly seated themselves and waited for the prayer to end. When the pastor lifted his head, he announced that the service was concluded and dismissed the congregation. That service had begun early, too! The people were friendly and offered to escort the two couples to another church, but they decided they'd had enough. They found out later that the services were held early due to the excessive heat.

AT HOME WITH THE RITCHEYS

Clyde and Esther lived in an apartment in Portage during the first few years of their marriage. During that time they had three daughters, Lillian, Elda, and Norma. Clyde was a very indulgent father. He opened a charge account at a local store that sold candy and ice cream, and told the owner, "Anything that my girls want they are allowed to have. Just record it and I'll pay it at the end of the week or on payday." That practice quickly ended when one day Lillian came running into the house crying and Esther found out that a girl connected to the store had carried her loudly protesting daughter into the store and tried to force her to buy something she didn't want.

Lillian remembered that her mother had a large red rocking chair set up in the kitchen of their first home. She would place a large pillow on the chair and tie Lillian into the chair, then make a sling from a diaper so Lillian could safely hold baby Elda so she wouldn't fall. Then, as Esther ironed clothes, she would rock the chair with her foot and sing songs to entertain the girls.

Around 1926, Clyde bought a house on Conemaugh Avenue, which had temporarily housed The Christian and Missionary Alliance Church. He paid

$4,000 for the house, using savings he had accumulated during his four and a half years in the Cavalry and his earnings as a coal-miner. The banks crashed three years later in 1929, the most devastating stock market crash in American history. If his savings had been in the bank, Clyde would have lost everything. As it was, the rapidly growing Ritchey family was fortunate to own and live in a house free of debt at a time when money was scarce. It was the beginning of the Great Depression.

Clyde may not have been a tall man at five feet, seven and a half inches in height, but he was powerfully built with a 48-inch barrel chest. He was a hard worker and often worked double shifts in the coalmine in order to provide for his large family. He felt it below his dignity to take welfare of any kind, especially since he was capable of providing for his family in his own way. He never went into debt, and set by example strong life principles for his children.

Working in a coalmine for 45 years aged Clyde quickly. He suffered painful rheumatism from all those years in the mines. But Clyde had a large family to support and was glad for every bit of pay he could earn. There were many mornings when Clyde would awaken early and walk over the mountain to help with the work on the farm, and then hitch a ride with his brother Alvin who also worked in the coalmines. When he got home at night, he would go to the basement to shower off all the coal dust, and then helped Esther get supper on the table. In fact, some days he would cook the entire meal to give Esther a break. When dinner was on the table, he'd call up the stairs to his children, "Come down and get it while it's hot, or I'll throw it out!"

One Saturday, the owner of the mines had a large order to fill and needed someone to load a coal hopper, which held a minimum of 50 tons of coal. It was Saturday, and he couldn't find enough men to do the job, so the mine owner came to Clyde. Whether it was Saturday or not, Clyde couldn't refuse the opportunity to earn extra money. Clyde told him, "If you provide the mules and someone to transport the coal out of the mine, I'll load that car full for you in one day." The man said, "You're crazy! No one man could possibly load that much coal in one day. You've got to shoot it (dynamite it), pick it, and shovel it into the mine cars. That's a big operation." Clyde said, "I can do it." The man responded, "I'll bet you $15 that you can't do it." Clyde took him up on it—he wasn't a Christian at that time, so he didn't have any qualms about betting. Besides, $15 was a lot of money in those days! Six hours after Clyde had begun work, the boss sent someone into the mine, saying, "Tell that d---fool to get out of the mines before he kills himself!" The coal hopper was already full—in only six hours.

His children had fond memories of Saturday mornings, when Clyde would get up and make breakfast. He'd load the table with griddlecakes or buckwheat pancakes, fried sausage, gravy, fried

19

"pudding" (or scrapple), eggs, and a big pan full of fried potatoes. He expected his children to clean their plates—there was to be no waste in a day when food was hard to come by. He loved to cook, and his daughters considered him to be the better cook—not that Esther wasn't a good cook! But her specialties were delicious desserts. She'd make ten to twelve pies each Saturday, and by Sunday night, the pies would all be gone, eaten by her children and their friends.

In the summers Clyde would take Bud with him to Blue Knob, walking eight miles over the mountain and back. They would pick blueberries and huckleberries from the little mountain bushes they found along the way for pies and preserves. Working on the farm also kept their family supplied with fresh farm produce, milk, and eggs. Sometimes they would bring a gun to hunt for squirrel, pheasant, and other small game along the way. In this way Clyde helped to amply provide for his family during the Depression. Not everyone appreciated all this homegrown bounty, however. His children were envious of their friends, who mixed yellow food coloring with oleomargarine so it looked like butter.

There were hard times to be experienced during the Depression, but the children learned to appreciate the small things in life, and it didn't take a lot to make them happy. Life was not complex in those days. There was a "Mayberry" quality to living, when neighbors frequently stepped over next door to borrow or return items they had borrowed, children freely roamed the neighborhood, and entertainment was where one found it.

During the Depression, the Ritcheys shared what they had with their neighbors. Clyde's philosophy was, "If you don't give your best to someone in need, you haven't really given anything." This attitude was extended even to a stranger who might knock on their door for a handout. Clyde was often heard to say that they might be entertaining an angel unaware. This open-handed hospitality was an example to his children. The Ritchey door was open to anyone in need. There was always room for one more at the dinner table, and the table was frequently full as Clyde gave thanks for the meal—and if Clyde heard of anyone in need, he was quick to share what he had.

As a young man Clyde chewed tobacco and smoked cigars. He was not a Christian at that time, but he didn't discourage his family from attending church. One day he developed a high fever and swelling around his badly infected ears. After the doctor had done all he could, Clyde turned to his wife Esther and asked, "Do you believe in the power of God to heal?" When Esther affirmed that she did, he asked her to call for her pastor and ask him to pray for him. Esther sent for the pastor of the C&MA church in Portage who came over and laid his hands on Clyde, Sr., praying for his healing. God heard his prayer and Clyde was instantly healed. Because of this evidence of the power of God, Clyde accepted Christ as his Savior. Several weeks later he noticed that, while he no longer had a desire for tobacco, he still carried it about with him out of habit from many years of use. He threw it away and never again had a desire for tobacco.

As Clyde grew in the knowledge of God, his love for Him also grew—at times overwhelming him. He taught his women's Sunday school class with a large worn Bible in one hand and a kerchief in the other to wipe tears as they streamed down his face. His younger daughters were accustomed to seeing their father sitting in his armchair in the living room at home, reading the Bible with tears running down his face. Occasionally he would shout out, "Esther, come listen to this!" There was no doubt that Clyde and Esther shared a love for their Lord. This love was passed on to their children.

Since Clyde was not a Christian in the early years of their marriage, Esther was the parent who had seen to the spiritual teaching of her children. A neighbor wrote years later, "Your mother was the one who looked into the future and saw the ability of her children. Through the church a seed was planted, but it takes a good gardener to nurture that seed and your mother was a good gardener."

Clyde was a strict disciplinarian who usually disciplined his children on the spot. This practice was something that his son vowed never to practice with his own children, as he felt it was not always fairly administered. But Clyde also freely administered love. In fact, there was a lot of love and laughter in the Ritchey home. The children witnessed first hand the love between their father and mother. It was not uncommon to find Esther standing at the kitchen sink, singing or whistling as she washed the dishes, when Clyde would steal up behind her to give her a kiss. My grandmother Esther once told me that during the day her time was devoted to her children, but at night, "Clyde knew I was all his." Dad told of many times coming home at night after a date, finding his parents sitting in the living room, with his mom on his dad's lap, arms around each other, her head on his shoulder, and they'd be sound asleep.

A BOY FROM THE NORTH

Dad was the Ritchey's fourth child and first son. He was the first of their nine children to be born in their new home. Esther was a small woman—only about four feet, ten inches tall—yet she gave birth to nine children—all of them big babies. In fact her second child was ten pounds at birth. Her husband used to tease Esther that the reason she had so many babies was that she got jealous each time a neighbor had a baby. Clyde was proud of all his children, but Esther was thrilled to finally present a son to her husband after three daughters.

Esther spent a long time deliberating over a name for her son. She kept mentioning ideas to Clyde who adamantly rejected them one by one. Finally one of her sisters told her, "You know, Esther, I think Clyde wants you to name the baby after him." After a few more names were rejected, Esther asked, "Clyde, how about if we name the baby after you?" To which Clyde indifferently replied, "Name him whatever you want. I don't care." Thus, the new baby boy was named Joseph Clyde Ritchey, Jr. after his proud father—nicknamed "Bud" so as not to be confused with his dad. My aunts related that their mother, in a private moment following Bud's birth, lay in bed and silently dedicated her son to God. She prayed, "Lord, if you want, you can take and use him on the mission field in darkest Africa."

Bud was a typically active boy of his day. Life growing up with a bunch of sisters was certainly different than if he had grown up with a bunch of brothers. He had chores, as did his sisters, but his chores mostly involved the outdoors, bringing coal in from the coalhouse, digging out the basement, spading up the garden, feeding the chickens, cleaning the chicken house, mowing the lawn with a push mower, and shoveling ice and snow off the walks in the wintertime. If he ever had to wash dishes it was as punishment.

He loved playing outdoors with his friends, accompanying his father on hunting or fishing trips, and working alongside his father when they went out over the mountain to Blue Knob to work on the family farm. An older sister remembered their dad coming up the sidewalk, carrying Bud on his shoulders when Bud's little legs couldn't carry him anymore. Esther would scold Clyde, Sr., "That poor little fellow! You had to drag him all through those woods!"

When Bud was around the age of three, his father made a little table with red rocking chairs for the children to set outside and play. He also had given Bud his own miniature set of working tools, with a little hatchet, a saw, and a hammer. One day some friends of the family came to visit. Because it was a special occasion, his oldest sister Lillian was allowed to entertain their little girl at the little table with one of her favorite dolls. When dinner was ready, the girls left the doll at their play area and went in to eat. When they returned they found total destruction. Bud had used his tools to cut up everything in sight: the legs and rungs on the little chairs and the table— and he had amputated the head and legs of the beautiful baby doll. How Lillian cried! Bud was punished, of course.

When Bud was four, he was in the basement with his father who was getting ready for work. His mother was also in the basement, doing laundry, and had just taken a load of wet laundry upstairs to hang up outside on the lines to dry. Bud decided that he was going to help Mom with the laundry. He climbed up on a stool, picked up a handkerchief that had been soaking in the washing machine and began to feed it through the old wringer. The wringer didn't have a safety release like later models had; it was the kind that you clamped down until it had the pressure you wanted. Next thing he knew, his fingers started going through with the cloth. His father heard him yell, and came running. He gave a powerful swing of his fist, knocking the wringer apart and sending it and Bud flying. By that time, his arm had gone in the wringers up to his elbow and the rollers had begun to pull the skin off his arm.

Clyde rushed his son to Dr. Daugherty, the family doctor. Bud's arm was as flat as a pancake. His father thought Bud's bones were crushed. Dr. Daugherty assured them that Bud's arm was not broken, and that it would fill out again.

The doctor examined the woeful little boy's face and asked what he wanted most in the world. After having three older sisters and then a fourth sister, he said, "I want a brother." Dr. Daugherty said, "Well, I tell you what. In a few months, you are going to have a brother." His prediction was undoubtedly rash considering that at that time, Bud was the only boy in a family of five children. Several months later, when his mother gave birth to a boy, Irvin, Bud just knew that it was all because of him. Irvin belonged to him because a brother was what the doctor promised him. He got three more sisters after that.

With nine children in the family, there was always plenty of mischief and activity. But there was also time to sit and relax on the front porch in the evenings, listening to crickets, and visiting with neighbors over the fence. The children played games in the street under the street lamps, churned home-made ice cream, or hid under the Hungarian Hall to watch the lively Catholic family dances.

Bud's friend's father ran the Hungarian Hall, and after the dances on Saturday night, his friend would sweep up all the cigarette butts, cigars, and pipe tobacco, and take it all home to grind up and make homemade cigarettes. One day, Bud's parents planned to leave on a day trip and Bud wanted to go with them. He threatened to go to his friend's house and smoke cigarettes all day if he couldn't go. They left without him, so Bud went to his friend's house, and they sat and smoked homemade cigarettes. Pretty soon Bud began to feel sick.

By the time Bud's parents returned home, he had thrown up and was a pretty miserable boy. His father sent one of his sisters after kindly old Dr. Daugherty. The doctor must have had an idea of the cause of Bud's sickness because he told Mom and Dad to go on downstairs and leave Bud with him. After awhile, the wise old man came downstairs and said, "I don't want you to say anything to that boy. He's already been punished. But you don't have to worry about him. There's nothing really seriously wrong. All he was doing was smoking. He was just trying it, and he got his punishment, so don't punish him."

Christmas was always a good time at the Ritchey home, even if they didn't have a lot of things under the tree. It was good, except for one year! This Christmas money was especially tight. But Bud wanted a pair of boxing gloves so much he could taste it. If he didn't get boxing gloves, he didn't care if he got anything! His older sisters knew that their father couldn't afford such an extravagance that year, so they decided to play a trick on him. On Christmas morning Bud looked anxiously under the tree, and lo and behold, there was a brightly wrapped box just the right size for boxing gloves! He eagerly unwrapped the box—and found two rolls of toilet paper. Deeply disappointed, and a little bit angry, he left the house. Seeing how deeply their prank had affected their brother, his sisters were ashamed and had difficulty enjoying the remainder of the day.

As a child, Bud went to the altar on numerous occasions. He came from a strong Armenian background and was taught he could be saved many, many times. The sad thing is that no one followed up on these occasions. The adults would simply pat Bud on the back and tell him he was a good boy. No one ever challenged him to examine his commitment to the Lord. In spite of the many times Bud went forward, the true implication of a life changed by Christ was lost to him. Fear that he would die and go to hell plagued him throughout his growing-up years, no doubt motivating his going forward for salvation so many times. Even through his high school years and the years before his true conversion, there was the fear that death would catch up with him.

Although he was not a "bad" boy during his growing years, Bud used a lot of slang words as most boys do—and swear words when his parents could not hear him. But never did Bud use the Lord's name in vain. There was an inner "brake" that kept him from going that far. Through his many boyhood experiences of conversion, his tongue did not change. Also, there were things Bud liked to do that he knew were wrong. He enjoyed going to the movies at a time when a Christian never went to the movies. In fact, there were times when he and his friends would sneak into the movie theater so they wouldn't have to pay.

On one occasion Bud took his younger brother

Irvin to the movies. Irvin was somewhat reluctant to go since he was trying to be a faithful Christian, but Bud talked him into it. Part way through the movie Irvin jumped up and ran out. He was afraid that Jesus would come back to earth that night and catch him doing something he knew was wrong, and he feared that he wouldn't go to heaven. This reflected on the teaching they had received at that time—that one's actions determined whether or not one would go to heaven—thus fueling the fear Bud carried with him. Yet, in spite of this fear, Bud continued to do the things he knew were wrong. He had the fear of God without experiencing the power of God to change his life.

DAYS OF WAR

Bud was a freshman in high school in 1941, when World War II broke out. December 7, the day Japan bombed Pearl Harbor, was a day he would never forget. It was as if the world had shifted on its axis. Everyone sat around radio sets listening for the latest word on the War.

Bud watched as his uncles and men from the area went off to war. There were not many men left in the surrounding cities and communities. All of the girls had boyfriends in uniform. In fact, his three older sisters each dated and later married servicemen. To an impressionable teenager, all this focus on the War bore with it an aura of excitement and romance. Bud could just visualize himself in the midst of it all—a hero of course!

Bud was enthralled by the reports of the War and during his senior year of high school gave thrilling reports of current events in his Problems of Democracy class. Each time Bud stood up to give a report, his teacher (who was also his principal) would enthusiastically prod him, "Keep going! Keep going!" One day his teacher pulled him aside and said, "Bud, I think you'd make a good preacher! I could listen to you speak all day!" At that particular time, being a preacher was the farthest thing from Bud's mind!

What the teacher didn't know was that Bud fancifully embellished current events with dramatic stories of fighter pilots and submarines, adding to what were already sensational events.

As a senior Bud began to think about his future. The only future he could envision for himself at that time was of going off to war. However, there were many signs that the War was not going to last much longer, and Bud was afraid he was going to miss being a part of it.

After high school, in the summer of 1945, Bud took the train to Pittsburgh, accompanied by one of his older sisters, with the intention of joining the Navy. He was informed that if he joined at that time he would be committed to the Navy for four years. Bud was taken aback. He thought to himself, "Man, if the war ends soon, I'll be stuck with the full four years!" He asked if there was a branch of the service that required less of a commitment in time. The Navy recruiter suggested the Merchant Marines. Because he was only seventeen, his father had to go with him to sign up.

At that time the Merchant Marines was a military branch of the Coast Guard. The Marines' slogan was "We Deliver the Goods." They carried troops, food, fuel, guns, machinery of war, and supplies to the various locations of the war. In fact, the U.S. Merchant Marines made a most significant contribution to winning the Second World War. Faced by danger from torpedoes, submarines, kamikaze pilots, and mines, the percentage of Merchant Marines who died in World War II was one in 24, greater than in any other branch of the service. Bud personally knew of men from his own hometown who had given their lives for their country while serving in the Merchant Marines.

Before Bud left for boot camp his father pulled him aside for a talk. "Now son," he said, "I spent nearly five years in the military back in World War I and I want to tell you about the things you are going to face out there." He was very frank as he described to his son the temptations of gambling, prostitutes, alcohol, and smoking would offer, as well as all the other temptations that would come his way. Then he said, "Son, you've been brought up right. You know the right way, and I have faith in you that you won't allow any of these things to touch your life. The decisions you make and the things you do hereafter will reflect on the way your mother and I raised you."

When Bud joined the service he found that everything his father had warned him about was true. This was the first time Bud had been away from home, and he also found that he was very homesick.

While at boot camp in Sheepshead Bay, New York, Bud began to think about spiritual things. In his search for an answer to his inner searching, he attended chapel on the base and also visited the Mormon Tabernacle in New York City with his new best friend Marvin Hoyt, a Mormon from Orderville,

Utah. This was a unique experience for Bud who did not hear preaching against sin such as he was accustomed to hearing in his church back home. Around this time he also visited a Catholic church with a friend, mimicking all the rituals his friend performed during the mass. But it didn't matter where Bud went or what he did; he received no true spiritual understanding or fulfillment.

During the Christmas holidays Bud came down with strep throat and ended up in a military hospital. There he met a young man named George Stebbins who taught Bud to play blackjack and poker, games that Bud grew to love to play. Unfortunately, they took a real hold in his life.

Toward the end of Bud's time in boot camp, word came over the airwaves on August 6, 1945, that the atomic bomb had been dropped on Hiroshima in Japan. Japan was now staggering, and everyone knew the end of the War was near. Three days later when the second bomb was dropped on Nagasaki, Japan surrendered. The War was over, except for the cleaning up after the war. The youthful Bud would teasingly claim that when the enemy heard he was coming they quit fighting.

When Bud got out of boot camp, he still had to fulfill the remainder of his contracted time of one year with the Merchant Marines. He was assigned to a troop ship headed to Antwerp, Belgium, sent to bring troops back from Europe. His companions on the troop ship were a rough bunch, hard-drinking and hard-living. His father's parting word came back to strengthen his resolve many times, but never more so than while he was in Belgium. He found himself in a very foreign world—a place of total destruction and depravity.

The now silent machinery of war lined the shattered streets. What had once been flourishing and productive factories were now piles of rubble, leveled by bombs. Half-tracks and tanks were loaded on warships and dumped in the ocean. Bud's companions would remain on shore at night to get drunk or find a prostitute. At times Bud was the only one who returned to the ship. Other times he would assist friends too drunk to navigate the trip back to the ship. On occasion he would sign in on the docket and take the place of a friend who had stayed on shore that should have been on ship. He knew this was wrong but he was trying to cover up for his friends so they wouldn't get in trouble.

The return to the States in February of 1946 was frightful. There were still mines in the ocean left undetected by mine sweepers. The dangers were made very real when a ship not too far behind the one he was on hit a mine while going through the English Channel. And the seas on the northern return route near Greenland and Iceland were very rough. The high waves sometimes crashed over the ship. At times the ship seemed to make little headway. The propeller of the ship would rise completely out of the water, shaking the whole ship as though to tear it apart. The speed of the ship had to be slowed so it wouldn't be destroyed.

Bud's job as an oiler kept him down in the hold of the ship. It was at times like this, scared and horribly seasick, that Bud found himself down on his knees in a dark corner, crying out, "Oh, God, if you bring me safely out of this, I'll do anything You want." He made many promises to God on that terrifying journey, yet when he got back safely on shore in New York, he forgot those promises.

A CHANGE OF HEART

When Bud returned home, he turned over his service pay to his father to help with the expenses at home. He renewed friendships with some of his young buddies who hadn't been in the service, and they ran around together. Bud got a job with a building contractor. Two of his future brothers-in-law had completed their terms in the service and joined him. Together they began to learn the building trade—skills that Bud would put to use many times throughout his life.

During this time Bud attended church occasionally to see a certain young lady who came from a good Christian family. Bud was by no means a faithful churchgoer, but the girl's parents lived too far out of town for him to visit easily or often, and the most convenient time and place he would be certain to see her was in church.

In October of 1946, revival services were being held in the Portage Alliance Church. Bud attended each night, knowing that the girl would be there. One night when she didn't show up, Bud actually listened to the message. He was greatly moved by what he heard and raised his hand for prayer when the invitation was given. Not quite ready to make a full commitment, Bud left immediately after the service.

His head was whirling as he walked the streets, weighing what he would have to give up against what he might gain if he accepted Christ as his Savior. The internal struggle was a tough one. He knew a decision was demanded of him, but he didn't know if he could give up all the things he loved—among them going to the movies and playing cards. The only benefit he could see to accepting Christ was the end of his lifetime fear of dying without Christ and going to hell. He finally decided that he couldn't give up the things of the world that had such a hold on him.

Sunday night was the last night of the revival services. Rather than taking a chance of coming under conviction once more, Bud decided to go to the movies. While standing in line waiting to get his ticket, he felt a tremendous pressure building up inside. He had a feeling that if he did not go to the service that night he would be eternally lost—that this would be his last chance at receiving salvation. It seemed as if a giant hand took hold of his body and pointed him toward the church. He began to walk. Almost involuntarily, Bud turned up the street toward the church, walked up the steps to the front doors, entered the sanctuary, and sat down on the first available seat closest to the aisle. He didn't want anything between him and the aisle when the invitation was given.

Bud didn't look for his girl. He didn't even pay attention to the message. All he knew was that when the invitation was given that night he was going to be the first one on his knees down at the altar. That night real revival broke out in the Portage Alliance Church. Later Bud found that his mother, a sister, a friend, and a number of others had also joined him at the altar. With joy bursting from his heart, Bud went home that night to awaken his father and tell him that his prayers for his son had been answered.

Four years later, in a testimony he wrote for a college newsletter, Bud wrote: "My heart cried out to God as I went forward to the altar that night, and Christ was faithful to His promise to save me if I confessed my sins unto Him. The joy and peace that flooded my soul was indescribable, and praise His name, He has never taken it away."

Bud's life was radically changed from that moment on. His desires for the things of the world were taken away. He no longer spoke foul language. He began to take Christ seriously. The revival service marked the beginning of a real moving of the Holy Spirit in the Portage Alliance Church. His cousin Ray Stombaugh came home from the military service about that time and the two young men began to hold cottage prayer meetings in the homes of the young people. As a result, the young people's group began to grow. They stood on street corners to preach and witness. They went to other towns to help other Alliance churches, going out with the pastors to hold street meetings. People were being saved right on the streets as young people joyously witnessed to the power of God to change lives. The young people held rallies, and in the summer they attended church camp. It was at Mahaffey Camp that Clyde heard about something called the deeper Christian life.

In his second year as a Christian, desiring a deeper walk with Christ, Bud went forward at Mahaffey and received the infilling of the Holy Spirit. He later claimed that this experience was as wonderful as his experience of salvation. He knew at that moment that he was truly filled with the Holy Spirit of God. His family witnessed a renewed enthusiasm and dedication of Bud's life toward Christ. Bud truly fell in love with his Savior—a love that never left him.

During this time Bud and his cousin Ray began to discuss the possibility of preparing for Christian ministry. They asked their pastor who had attended Nyack Missionary Training Institute if he would accompany them to Nyack to check it out. At Nyack Bud was surprised to find an old acquaintance— George Stebbins, the young man who had taught him to play cards while he was in the service. It turned out that George, brother of Thomas Stebbins, missionary to Vietnam, had wandered away from God for a time. But God had gotten hold of George's life and now he was preparing for ministry as a student at Nyack.

Later Ray and Bud also decided to attend Nyack where they would train to serve the Lord.

ENTER THE GIRL FROM THE SOUTH

Doris Virginia Hoover was a good Southern girl, born in South Georgia and raised in Florida. Her parents were Harold Herbert Hoover and Ethel Blanche Luke Hoover.

Doris's mother Ethel was born prematurely on August 12, 1906, in south Georgia to Margaret (Maggie) and Richard (Dick) Luke. She was the ninth of thirteen children. The two and a half-pound baby lay on the pillow next to her mother, struggling for life, drawing warmth from the heated bricks that surrounded her. Chances were slim that the baby would survive. Her mother lay in bed recovering from the baby's birth, resignedly sewing a tiny white burial dress with puffed sleeves and lace inserts. She had already prepared a size three shoebox, lined with white satin for the baby's burial. But the indomitable spirit of her pioneer ancestors was alive in the small baby. Ethel Blanche Luke lived. Ethel was two before she could walk and was small for her age throughout her early childhood. However, her size did not exempt her from working alongside her brothers and sisters in the tobacco and cotton fields on the home farm. In time she caught up in size with others her age.

At age 20 Ethel left the home farm in South Georgia to move in with a sister in Daytona Beach, Florida. She got a job working at Slylings Ice Cream Plant. On New Year's Day, 1927, her friend Eula Dees introduced her to a young man, Harold Herbert Hoover.

Harold was born in Harrisburg, Pennsylvania, on December 16, 1903, to Frank E. Hoover and Clara Sevilla Kinsinger Hoover. Before Harold's fourteenth birthday, four members of his family had died. While a younger brother had died of diphtheria earlier, Harold's father and two older sisters—one was married—died of the influenza virus within a two-week period. The soldiers of World War I had unknowingly carried the deadly "Spanish Influenza" epidemic around the world. Twenty million people worldwide died of this epidemic between 1918-1919. In her time of overwhelming grief, Clara, a first generation American, found she could no longer stay in a home painfully alive with the memories of loved ones who were no longer with her. She gathered her belongings and three young sons and moved as far away from Harrisburg, Pennsylvania as she could go. She ended up in Bunnell, Florida.

Harold, Walter, and young Charlie lived with their mother in a rooming house where she held the job of housekeeper. One of the boarders, Mr. Harry Booe, took an interest in the widow and her three sons. He taught her sons his trade and offered the eldest, Harold, a job painting houses with him. Clara and Harry were married and her sons now had a new father. Harold and his brothers later started their own business, "The Hoover Brothers," as housepainters.

On June 8, 1927, six months after they met, Ethel and Harold were married in Deland, Florida. Harold continued to work as a house painter after they were married. The Depression years were upon them. Work was scarce and the Hoovers moved around to wherever they could find jobs. When Ethel found that she was pregnant, they decided to move back to Lenox, Georgia, where Ethel would have the help of her family and the attention of doctors she knew. Richard Franklin Hoover was born November 28, 1928. A little over a year later on January 20, 1930, Doris Virginia Hoover was also born in Lenox. Ethel and Harold continued to travel between Florida and South Georgia, going wherever jobs could be found. Years later, Ethel carried memories of standing in long welfare lines with one child on her hip and the other hanging on her skirts.

When Dick was three years old, the Hoovers finally settled back in Daytona Beach. It was there that Margaret Clara Hoover was born on January 22, 1935, in the new Halifax Hospital in Daytona Beach. Harold worked off the bill of $50 for a ten-day maternity stay by helping to give the new hospital its first coat of paint. After the bill was paid, Harold continued to work there. The growing hospital provided the Hoover brothers with painting jobs for many years.

People thought Dick and Doris were twins since they looked so much alike. Ethel had tried to start

Dick in first grade when he was five, but he had difficulties adjusting and Ethel withdrew him from school. Entrance requirements were not as strict as they are today, and Dick was just too young. The next year Ethel decided it would be less trouble for her to have both Dick and Doris begin school at the same time rather than having to go through two separate adjustment periods with the children. Doris started first grade in the same class with her brother, even though she would not be six until the following January.

Doris was even less prepared for school than Dick had been the year before. She was immature and did not want to be in school. Her mother had to cut a switch and follow along behind Doris for the first block or two on the way to school. Doris would be tearful by the time she reached school. She didn't understand the material, and had difficulty keeping up. Doris responded to her frustrations by crying. She spent a lot of time sitting by herself in the cloakroom, having been sent there by the teacher so her crying wouldn't disrupt the other children. She only passed first grade because she could read well. But the trauma of her first year of school stayed with Doris for many years. Just the smell of chalk or the sight of a page with the largely spaced lines for printing would bring back a flood of memories that would cause her to shudder. By junior high school she finally felt comfortable in school and began to fit in enough to enjoy herself.

The pastor of a nearby church took an interest in the Hoover children and other children in the neighborhood. Each Sunday, Rev. and Mrs. A. Paul McGarvey would drive around the neighborhood, picking up children at play, and bringing them to the Daytona Beach Christian and Missionary Alliance Church on Ridgewood Avenue. Some of the children, including Dick and Doris, would be barefoot and in their dusty play clothes, but the McGarveys brought them anyway and seated them on the front pew of the church.

When Doris was around 11, she and her brother Dick attended evangelistic meetings at their church. Their mother and father did not attend church regularly at that time, and Margaret was young enough to still be at home with her mother. Doris sat next to her Sunday school teacher and when the invitation was given, her teacher leaned over and asked, "Doris, would you like to go forward?" Doris nodded. Her teacher gave her a little push. Doris went forward and the pastor led her in prayer as she accepted Christ as her Savior. She and Dick were baptized later that year.

Out of the many children the McGarveys brought to church were a number who ended up serving the Lord as adults. Tom Bozeman and his wife became C&MA missionaries to Irian Jaya. Polly Bozeman Bowman served with her husband as C&MA missionaries in Mali. Becky Moberg Wellings and her husband were missionaries to Niger. Bob Bozeman and

Dick Hoover became C&MA pastors. And of course, Mom (Doris) would later serve as a missionary to Ivory Coast with Dad.

While in high school, Doris took commercial courses to prepare herself for working in the business world. However, as graduation neared, Doris felt a desire to follow the Lord's direction for her future, whatever that might be. By this time she had some experience teaching children in Sunday school and had been active in the young people's work in her church, doing visitation and ministering to others. Her pastor had graduated from Nyack Missionary Training Institute and influenced many of the young people of his church to attend Nyack. A major in Christian Education appealed to Doris, so she applied to attend Nyack. However, Nyack would not accept a student under the age of 18, so Doris worked as a cashier in a store for a year after graduating from high school before leaving for Nyack.

THE BUMPY ROAD TO LOVE

(Note: Dad is now known by "Clyde," rather than his childhood name of "Bud.")

When Doris arrived at Nyack in the fall of 1948, she found all the students, whether or not they were mission majors, joined in missionary prayer bands to pray for and support missions. Doris felt no special call to be a missionary, nor leanings toward any certain country or continent. However, if she had, it probably would have been in Africa. But her roommate, noting that the African prayer band already had a great many members while other prayer bands had only a few, suggested they join the India prayer band, which was very small.

Clyde and his cousin Ray entered Nyack that same year and they also joined a prayer band—the Africa prayer band. In early October revival services were held at Nyack. Clyde wrote home: "There wasn't a person who went to the altar until Wednesday evening. That's when the break came. With no altar call given, the Spirit of God truly worked. There were at least 100 young people at the altar that night. The testimonies were wonderful afterwards. Some were shocking. There were those here who were studying the Word of God and had never been saved. Others had things in their lives they knew were not pleasing to God. But the greatest thrill of all was the way the Holy Spirit filled the hearts of those who were wholly consecrated to Him. My own spirit was revived and I got a completely new vision of Jesus this week. I love Him more now than ever before. I'll never be able to thank Him enough for what He has done for me. I can't understand why He has blessed me in the many ways that He has. I know that I am not worthy of His blessings."

Clyde felt the Lord was leading him toward the mission field. He heard a missionary from Gabon speak and felt that perhaps the Lord was calling him to work among the pygmies of that country. While still at Nyack, Clyde and Ray made application to go to the mission field with The Christian and Missionary Alliance. Clyde listed Gabon as the country of his choice while Ray simply noted, "anywhere in Africa." Later they found it ironic that when the appointments were made, Ray was sent to Gabon and Clyde was sent "anywhere in Africa"—the Ivory Coast.

In the spring of 1951, before graduation, Clyde participated in an event that would further prepare him for the spiritual battles ahead. He wrote home: "We have had quite an interesting event take place here at the school this weekend. The only reason I tell it is so the glory of God might be seen in it. A lady here at school was possessed with demons. Her condition was so bad that she was bedfast. I saw four of the demons cast out of her last night and it was a blood-curdling experience. We sang songs about the blood of Jesus and the demons went into a rage. The way they talked was inhuman. But praise God, at the command 'In Jesus Name,' the demons had to flee. They tried their best to keep her body, but God is Victor. You'll never know how much the songs *There is Power in the Blood,* and *All Hail the Power of Jesus' Name* mean to me now. To have seen the power of God over the forces of darkness was wonderful. As believers in Christ we can praise God that He who is in us is greater than he that is in the world."

Clyde worked at a box factory in Nyack to support himself while in college. This factory provided jobs for many of the students through the years. Clyde brought his homework with him, studying during his breaks. In his senior year Clyde was promoted to in-spector. This promotion provided more study time and a larger salary, which enabled Clyde to anony-mously help other students. But life at college was not all work and study—there was also time for leisure activities. Clyde enjoyed college life, being with his friends, attending school events, or going into town. He did not do a great deal of dating, al-though his prankster cousin Ray set him up on dates a few times without his previous knowledge or con-sent.

In their junior year, Doris Hoover and Clyde Ritchey began to date. Clyde had not been dating anyone at the time and Doris caught his eye. She was popular on campus, and his friends prodded him to ask her out. He was intrigued by her and decided to take his chances and ask Doris out. He invited her to go with him to Jack Wyrtzen's Youth for Christ meetings in New York City. She admired Clyde and thought he was a nice guy, so she agreed to go with him. But while Clyde was interested in furthering a serious relationship, Doris wanted to be just friends. After dating a few times they agreed to go their separate ways, dating other people. Clyde was deeply disappointed.

That summer Clyde remained at Nyack to work and take a summer class, while Doris returned to Daytona Beach to work at a Howard Johnson's. In a letter to Doris, he hinted of his disappointment, "When I think of the swell fellowship I have had with you here at school I can't help but wish it could have continued. It's too bad the woman always has the last word. (I'm only kidding—or am I?) I'd better close for now before I ruin everything."

Ever hopeful, toward the end of their senior year Clyde again asked Doris out. She agreed to go with him to the Fishers of Men banquet, but reminded him, "Clyde you know how I feel." Clyde was once again hurt and disappointed by her response and decided on the spot to not ask her out again. What Clyde did not know was that it was during this date that Doris realized that her feelings for him were changing. She was beginning to fall in love with him. Of course, she could not let him know, especially in a day when the man made all the moves; and he would not make any advances in their relationship because she had already made it clear she was not interested. After graduation they went their separate ways.

Before graduation Doris's roommate expressed her uncertainty concerning the future. She did not know what plans God had for her life. Doris felt the same way, but she knew she could trust God for His best for her. Doris and another friend, Mary Walker (later to be Mary Kadle, C&MA missionary to Ecuador) joined forces and were contacted by the C&MA District Superintendent for the large Southeastern District concerning ministry among children. Mary's friends gave them a car for use in ministry, and since Mary couldn't drive Doris did all the driving, until Mary eventually got her license. Their first appointments were for vacation Bible schools in Daytona Beach and then in Minneola, Florida. They conducted several vacation Bible schools throughout Florida that summer. When the school year started in the fall they traveled throughout the Southern states holding Child Evangelism Fellowship meetings.

That summer, while they were still in Daytona Beach preparing material for the first Bible school, Doris and Mary received a surprise visit from some old college friends.

Paul Alford and Clyde had met in the fall of 1948 as freshmen at Nyack and became close friends that first semester. Paul often went home with Clyde for breaks and was soon adopted by "Mom" Ritchey as one of her boys. He never forgot Mom Ritchey and her warm hospitality. Paul and Clyde shared an enthusiasm for evangelism and went out on Saturday afternoons to witness door to door with Fishers of Men, a college organization. They often preached on Sundays in nearby churches. Each served as president of the Missionary Committee for a semester during their senior year.

As graduation approached, Clyde and Paul began to make plans for their future. They had heard about some churches in New England, which had closed. They decided to go there for a month of evangelistic crusades after graduation and try to re-open two of the churches as Alliance churches, figuring that each would pastor one of these churches for their home service before going to the mission field.

However, while "man proposes, God disposes." God had other plans for these young men. Dr. T. G. Mangham, District Superintendent of the Southeastern District, approached Paul, who was from this district, concerning his plans following graduation. Dr. Mangham asked if they would consider going to plant an Alliance church in Albany, Georgia. The district would provide a tent and rent a lot for evangelistic meetings. The plan was that after a church was started, one of the young men could pastor the church while the other moved on to another church.

Clyde and Paul prayed about their decision and felt that God was leading them southward. They purchased a 1939 Buick from a friend for $158.00 and spent $25.00 on parts. Clyde made the repairs with Paul assisting. The car burned oil and they joked about stopping at the gas station for one quart of gasoline and five gallons of oil. They drove through the night since they had no money to stay in a hotel. As they drove south, they stopped frequently to put oil in the car, sometimes in the dead of night, holding a flashlight in their mouth so they could pour the oil into the right hole. They finally reached Paul's home in Tampa, Florida, where Paul's mother told them Dr. Mangham wanted them to call him immediately.

Plans changed again. It was not the right time to go to Albany since a group from Bob Jones was holding citywide meetings. However, a friend of theirs, Sam Ferrell, had just gone to Biloxi, Mississippi, and the church did not have enough money for an evangelist to hold special meetings. Would they be interested? They were.

Having a week free before their first service, and knowing Clyde's feelings concerning Doris, Paul suggested they look up Doris and Mary. Paul was already a happily engaged man and wanted to see his pal equally happy.

Paul mentioned to Clyde, "You know, Doris and Mary are supposed to be in Minneola. That's only an hour's drive away. Why don't we go over there just to say 'Hi?' "

Clyde responded, "No, if we go, she'll think I'm chasing her, and she already said she wasn't inter-

53

ested in anything permanent."

Paul said, "Oh, come on. It's not that far and we don't have anything else to do. Let's go." When they got to Minneola, they found out that Mary and Doris were in Daytona Beach.

Seeing doors slamming in his face, Clyde said decidedly, "Let's go back. We're sure not going all the way over to Daytona Beach! Then she'll really know I'm chasing her!" But Paul could be very persuasive, and he and Clyde ended up on Doris' doorstep.

It had only been a short time before that Doris had reminded him of how she felt, and Clyde did not have expectations of anything having changed on that front. That night, the four friends sat on the Hoover's front porch talking. They reminisced about school friends, discussed their plans for the summer, and talked about everything else that came to mind.

At 1:00 in the morning Paul went to bed, which happened to be on the couch under the window where Clyde and Doris were sitting. Paul became an unwitting but interested witness to the conversation that followed. By 3:00 Mary was in bed. Finally around 4:00, Clyde and Doris's conversation turned to the times they had dated at Nyack. Clyde commented, "Well, you can't help how you feel."

Doris returned hesitantly with, "Well, no, I can't help how I felt."

The use of the past tense took Clyde unawares. For the moment he was speechless. He knew that what he wanted of Doris was a full commitment to the life to which God had called him. He was going to be a missionary in Africa. If Doris was to be his wife—and that was his intention—she would have to make a sacrifice of her own plans and life. He cleared his throat and tentatively said, "Well, Doris, this could mean we'll spend our lives together in Africa."

"I'm willing," she wholeheartedly responded. Doris often reflected that this was her call to Africa. Her call was service to God, and since God had brought them together she was gladly willing to follow Clyde into ministry, wherever that might take her.

When Paul and Clyde left the next morning, Clyde was full of joyful anticipation of a future with his beloved Doris. Later that day, Clyde wrote in a letter to Doris: "When I think of all the time we seemed to have wasted it sort of irritates me. I have never felt toward a girl like I feel toward you, Doris. I do love you with all my heart and I mentioned last night I wish I had more to offer you. One thing we can rest assured in and praise God for is that 'All things DO work together for good to those that love God and are the called according to His purpose.' I learned valuable lessons of patience and trusting God more when I put you upon the altar some time ago. This has made me believe God for great things through the power of His Spirit in the future. I am greatly anticipating the work we are about to enter in. We know that, 'Faithful is He that called thee who will also do it.' His word is sweet and His promises precious as we walk arm in arm with Him."

In October Clyde bought a ring and returned to Daytona Beach to make the engagement official. He wanted to give the ring to her privately, but her little sister would not be packed off to bed. It got later and later, until finally Clyde gave in, and asked Doris's father, mother, and little sister for permission to marry Doris. When he received it, he finally placed the ring on her finger.

PREPARING FOR THE ADVENTURE

Clyde and Paul called Sam Ferrell and made arrangements to go to Biloxi, Mississippi, for two weeks. The opening Sunday there were only 13 in church—among them a husband and wife with their six children. They held evangelistic meetings during the first week. The second week they held a Bible school. On the closing night of Bible school there were over 100 in the church. While they were ministering in Biloxi, these two young enthusiastic workers also painted the front of the church and did general repairs around the property.

At the end of their two weeks of ministry in Biloxi, they called Dr. Mangham and found the Bob Jones meetings were continuing in Albany, but there was another church in Meridian, Mississippi, that couldn't afford an evangelist. The church had been praying for revival each day for six months. Were Clyde and Paul interested? They were.

They drove to Meridian, planning to spend two weeks with Rev. Walter Sandell. Walter had just completed a 40-day period of fasting and prayer, and conditions were ripe for God's blessing. Clyde and Paul ended up staying six weeks. When they arrived, there were only about 25 people in the congregation. The two young men went door to door, witnessing and inviting people to come to the special services. They took turns preaching with Clyde leading the singing and providing the special music. By the time they left Meridian, there were over 150 people meeting regularly in the church. The Lord was working in an unusual way in the lives of these two young men as He prepared them for the work He had for their futures.

Some of those who met the Lord in the meetings in Meridian invited the young evangelists to come hold meetings in their little town of Union, Mississippi. The churches in Union organized a week of citywide meetings held in the park. It was quite an experience for these two young evangelists.

They sold their old Buick to a man who came back to the Lord through the meetings in Meridian. This man later became an Assemblies of God pastor. Clyde and Paul then bought two old Chevrolets and used the parts from one to get the 1941 model running.

Walter and Margaret Sandell did not have transportation at that time, so Clyde and Paul drove them in October in their "new" car to the district prayer conference held at Toccoa Falls, Georgia. This was the first time Paul and Clyde had been to Toccoa Falls College (then, Toccoa Falls Institute). Doris and Mary were also at the prayer conference and it was there, at the beautiful Toccoa Falls that Clyde and Doris again committed to spend their lives together in marriage and in the service of their Lord.

The young couple enjoyed their stolen moments together, and Clyde later wrote Doris, "I miss you so much already and wish I could walk up to Toccoa Falls again this morning and have prayer with you. I love you for your sincerity and devotion to our Lord, honey. You will always be a challenge to me. I still think you are too good for me." Little did they know at that time that Toccoa would be the place to which they would one day retire.

Clyde, Paul, and the Sandells returned to Meridian. From Meridian, the young men packed their car and moved on to conduct evangelistic meetings in Daytona Beach, Florida; Hamilton, Alabama; and Lake Worth, Florida. Each door opened without advance advertising or planning. Clyde and Paul took turns preaching; they went door-to-door, held Bible schools, spoke on the radio, and Clyde often led the music or sang solos. God continued to bless their ministry as many people met the Lord.

It was while they were still in Meridian that Paul felt the Lord leading him to start an Alliance church in Columbus, Georgia. On December 29, Paul married and the young men parted ways. Paul and his bride Grace moved to Columbus. Paul was to serve the Lord in many capacities throughout his lifetime, including as an Alliance missionary in Ecuador, pastor in the Southeastern District, Superintendent of the Southeastern District, Vice President of The Christian and Missionary Alliance, and President of Toccoa Falls College.

Rev. Hann Browne, pastor of the Daytona Beach Alliance Church, suggested that Clyde plant an Alliance church in nearby Ormond Beach, Florida. Clyde was living with the Hoover family at that time, until he and Doris could get married. Clyde started with tent meetings in a borrowed district tent set up on a vacant lot. Because it was winter, there was a pot-bellied stove in the center of the tent for heat. He worked with Doris's brother Dick in a grocery store and in his spare time he went around the Ormond Beach area, knocking on doors and inviting people to come to church. In a very short time there was a sizable congregation meeting in the tent and it became apparent that the time had come to start building.

During that winter, Doris worked on wedding plans for February. One of their friends suggested that Clyde and Doris apply to be on the "Bride and Groom Show," a nationally televised program produced by CBS in New York City. As a lark, without any expectation of being accepted, they applied to appear on the show. In late January 1952, they were astonished to receive a telegram inviting them to be featured on the Bride and Groom Show. In February they headed north with Margaret and one of Margaret's friends and Rev. and Mrs. Hann Browne, pastor of the Daytona Beach Alliance Church who would perform the ceremony on February 28.

Clyde's parents, his cousin and best man Ray Stombaugh, and Rev. and Mrs. Wilbur Powell (pastor of the Portage Alliance Church), were also at the ceremony in the small television studio, as well as a few other friends who lived close enough to attend. The program was interrupted at intervals to advertise Hudson paper napkins, which would later provide a source of hilarity to the Ritchey's children who enjoyed viewing the marriage on the reel provided by CBS. Among the prizes awarded the couple at the end of the show were a wedding ring set, table silver, a vacuum cleaner, glassware, blankets, an electric dishwasher, and a gas range—and a year's supply of Hudson paper napkins. In addition, the newlyweds were provided with a new car to use on an all-expense paid honeymoon to Niagara Falls. After the ceremony, various members of the CBS staff, including the host, shared how they were touched by the testimony of this young couple, dedicated to spending their lives serving their God in Africa.

After their honeymoon at Niagara Falls, Doris and Clyde went to Portage, where the Ritchey family had arranged for a wedding reception in Clyde's childhood home. From there they returned to Florida to continue their work in Ormond Beach.

Clyde and Doris lived with old Mr. Fenty, a family friend who invited them to share his home. During that time, Clyde worked on building the Ormond Beach Alliance Church.

The building of the church in Ormond Beach was a steppingstone to building churches in Africa. The church began in a tent that belonged to the District.

Services were held every night and every day Clyde went out in visitation, inviting people to the services. One of their favorite evangelists at night was Rev. Hendon Brown of Toccoa Falls College. He came in the fall each year to preach. One of the founding members of the church had a father who died leaving her an inheritance. She gave $16,000 to buy property for the church and to begin building the two-story block building. The downstairs was used for services and Sunday school while the upstairs served as living quarters for the Ritcheys. During that first year over 100 people prayed for salvation.

At that time, two years of home service were required of missionary candidates by The C&MA before they went overseas as missionaries. However, since the work in Ormond Beach was a new church plant, Dr. Mangham suggested that Clyde give an extra year to the church in order to give the church some stability before passing it on to someone else. For three years Clyde held two services each Sunday and Bible study and prayer meeting each Wednesday night. Every other Thursday night a young people's Bible study class was held with the rapidly growing youth group. Besides church planting, Clyde also alternated speaking on a daily 15-minute radio program that he shared with another local preacher. Clyde also preached on a street corner every Saturday night for the Salvation Army. Many people were saved on that corner.

Clyde worked at different jobs since the church

was not yet organized and he needed to support his family. He also did plastering and other construction work. These jobs helped to give him the skills he would use many times while on the mission field. While looking for a full-time job, while roofing a building, hot tar was accidentally spilled on his arm. Clyde was rushed to the hospital, but they couldn't remove the hardened tar. Eventually the tar peeled off leaving behind the newly healed skin. During 1953 he worked full-time for Florida Power and Light. The foreman of the crew and a lineman and his wife were led to the Lord and became members of the Ormond church.

Clyde was always busy, but in spite of his schedule, he found ways to fit in a little "play" time. He had always enjoyed fishing and hunting, and fishing off the coast of Florida was just one of the many perks of living there. However, he discovered that fishing wasn't always pleasurable. One day Clyde was surf fishing from the beach and all he caught was an inedible ocean catfish. Frustrated, he gingerly removed the fish from the hook and kicked the catfish back into the water. The barb on the spine of the catfish went into his toe and broke off when the catfish went flying. That barb was very painful for a while. About a year later it finally worked its way out through the other side of his toe.

The Ritchey's first child was born on April 23, 1953, in the Halifax Hospital in Daytona Beach, Florida. Clyde had planned to name his firstborn (a son, of course) after his best friend and cousin, Ray Stombaugh. Officially, the name would be Raymond Robert Ritchey, but in good Southern fashion, Doris already had a nickname ready—"Ray-Bob." It is typical of Southern names to be either hyphenated, two names used as one, initials, or cornball—like "Bubba." When the baby turned out to be a girl, Doris had to hurriedly pick a name from a book while lying in bed in the hospital. Brenda Ruth Ritchey was a much better name for a daughter—and, thankfully (at least to me, their daughter), not normally abbreviated.

Later, in September that same year, Clyde and Paul Alford, as well as a number of other young pastors were ordained at the annual district prayer conference in Boca Raton, Florida.

The next year, when Doris discovered she was expecting a second child, she wrote to her in-laws in Pennsylvania that Clyde didn't know whether he dared hope for a son this time. Once again, Doris got to name the baby, this time for a friend at Nyack whose name she admired, Mary Kaye (Redpath) Pease. Naturally, this name would appeal to Doris, as it was a good Southern two-name name! Mary Kaye was born on September 24, 1954. She was a roly-poly butterball of a baby with large blue eyes. Clyde may have been disappointed at not having a son at that time, but he was certainly proud of his two daughters.

In June 1955, Clyde and Doris went to Philadelphia, Pennsylvania, to attend the Annual Council of The C&MA. While there they met others who made up the large group of young people going out as missionaries for the first time. This was one the largest groups of missionaries to go to the foreign mission fields since World War II ended. In August, the Ritcheys made their farewells to their loved ones in the States, first in Ormond Beach and Daytona Beach, Florida; then they went north to Clyde's hometown of Portage, Pennsylvania. After Portage they went to The C&MA headquarters in New York City where they participated in orientation for new missionaries.

The ship on which the Ritcheys were to travel was a luxury liner from the American Holland Lines. On board with the Ritcheys were a few other missionaries who were also headed to France for language study. As the missionaries boarded ship there was a large group of friends at the dock to see them off— some of them classmates from Nyack. As the ship set sail, the missionaries tearfully waved goodbye to the friends and family members on shore. There was an air of excitement mixed with sorrow at the thought of leaving loved ones behind. This soon changed to anticipation as the Ritcheys thought of the uncharted territories ahead of them with new lands, new cultures, and new languages.

THE ADVENTURE BEGINS

After disembarking from the ship in LeHavre, France, the Ritcheys boarded a train that took them to Paris. All of a sudden the realization sunk in that no one understood them, and worse, they didn't understand anyone—they were in a world of strangers with no way to communicate. They were thankful to be met in Paris at 10:00 that night by fellow language student Herb Nehlsen. French automobiles were very small and even at that time of night the traffic in Paris was terrible as the driver dangerously wove in and out of traffic at a high speed. They stayed at a hotel their first night. After a good night's sleep, they went back to the railroad station to collect their baggage. When everything had cleared customs, they hired a truck to move their baggage to the apartment Herb had rented for them.

Their apartment was on the second floor of a three-story house in a Paris suburb. The concierge (landlady) lived on the ground floor, and Lutheran missionaries to Madagascar (also studying French) were on the third floor. The back of the apartment overlooked a park where young men played soccer.

Clyde was delayed in registering for classes because shortly after he hit land, he was laid low by seasickness, reminding him of his days in the Merchant Marines. The ground under his feet was still rolling and it took several days for him to recover his "land legs." There was an hour of travel time each way to and from classes. In addition to their classes at the Alliance Française, Clyde and Doris shared a private tutor for an hour apiece each day. Clyde also took a course in linguistics at the Sorbonne while in Paris. Girls from the nearby Bible Institute would come over to baby-sit so Clyde and Doris could study. Brenda was two and a half, and Mary Kaye celebrated her first birthday soon after their arrival in France.

Doris was glad for each item she had brought to France. She soon had their small apartment looking like home. She discovered that the cheapest way to shop was to go to the open-air markets that were open three mornings a week. She was also thankful that Brenda had found a playmate in Danny, the little boy upstairs. When they sat down for their first meal in their new apartment Brenda announced, "Mommy, I like my new home."

There were many new customs to learn. Clyde and Doris noticed right away that, except for the main thoroughfares, people always walked in the middle of the road. They quickly discovered the reason—the sides of the road were used as a public bathroom. It was not uncommon to see an individual stop to relieve himself in plain view at the side of the road. Another custom to which they had to adjust was that people did their grocery shopping every day since so few had refrigerators. Doris avoided this inconvenience by renting a small refrigerator.

The landlady of the apartment building was an excellent housekeeper and kept the floors highly polished. One day, Clyde was going down the steps of the apartment house carrying Mary Kaye when he slipped on the newly polished steps. Unable to save both himself and the baby from injury, he held her up high in the air while he bumped down the steep stairs on his backside—a painful experience! Clyde went to the American hospital in Paris where exams revealed a large painful lump. Thankfully nothing was broken.

Clyde and Doris often attended church at the French Bible Institute in order to help their French. This was also an unusual experience since the program included monotonous chanting instead of the singing of hymns such as the Ritcheys were accustomed to hearing. Sometimes they attended the French Lutheran church with their upstairs neighbors. But it didn't matter which church they attended—they did not yet understand French.

On Sunday evenings they went in to Paris to visit a Missionary Orientation Center run by an elderly French couple. The center was open to all the new missionaries studying French who were invited for a potluck dinner and a service. This gave the language study students an opportunity to try out their French by giving a testimony or taking some part in the service. It was a safe place to make mistakes since the members of the audience were also struggling with French.

They soon began to attend an English-speaking church. As they began to sing to the accompaniment of the piano, Brenda began to cry. Each time a song was played she would cry. When the service was over Brenda told her parents that the music made her sad. What she was trying to say was that sound of the gospel singing made her homesick for America. When Doris asked her for whom she was homesick, Brenda answered, "Grandma." Grandma Hoover had been her babysitter on many occasions, and had watched Brenda and Mary Kaye while her parents were in ministry.

She wasn't the only one homesick so far away from home. Clyde noted in a letter to his mother, "I am convinced that homesickness is for people and not for a geographical location. When we obey God's call to go, we can expect Abraham's experience to be ours. We go out not knowing whither we go. We become pilgrims and strangers in a foreign land. I imagine the dining room table at home that used to be full to overflowing on Sundays is now rather vacant. If it's any comfort to you, our table is the same—but of course the children make a difference."

For their first Thanksgiving Day dinner away from the United States, the Ritcheys joined about 50 other American missionaries representing many denominations who were studying French at the American church in Paris. They enjoyed all the Thanksgiving trimmings they would have enjoyed back home. Before the meal they all stood and sang the doxology. Again, Brenda began to cry and said the song made her homesick.

In spite of homesickness, a different culture, and difficulties learning the language, Clyde was able to write home: "We again find our hearts full of praise to God for His manifold blessings to us this past week. We shouldn't judge God's blessings from the natural viewpoint, but from the spiritual. We thank God for the needs we have and the trials and tests we have been put through, for these only convince us more and more of our own insufficiency and of our dependence upon God. The language may always have its barriers, but we praise God for that which we understand and are able to speak. Our health is excellent and Christ has met every need. We could go on and on with our testimony of God's grace and power that has been our portion since coming to France. We don't by any means claim that there haven't been moments of discouragement and tears of supplication over the language—but these too have helped us understand and appreciate the struggle of missionaries down through the years. As always, God has chosen the foolish things, the weak things, the base things, things that are despised, things that are not, 'That no flesh should glory in His presence.' Our glory is and should be 'in the Lord.'"

One of the benefits of living in Europe was travel to nearby countries. During a vacation from studies, the Ritcheys went on a tour of Switzerland, Germany, Belgium, and the Netherlands with another young couple with whom they were studying. While in the Black Forest area, they bought a cuckoo clock that served them for many years in Africa.

Back in classes, concentrating on French lessons had their effect on Clyde. Doris woke up one night to find her spouse conjugating verbs in his sleep. "Je suis. Tu es. Il est. Elle est. Nous somme. Vous etes." One day they were invited to their French tutor's home for a meal. Monsieur Jeuteau was a professor of linguistics at the Berlitz. Since his breath always smelled of garlic—which Clyde could not abide—he decided in advance that he was going to be very careful about the food he ate. Doris had spent some time in the kitchen watching the tutor's wife finish food preparations and was appalled when she later observed Clyde helping himself to a large portion of deviled eggs. They looked harmless, and he never dreamed anyone would add garlic to deviled eggs. But Doris had seen how much garlic had gone into their preparation. Clyde manfully ate what he took, but from that time on had an even stronger aversion to garlic. Mr. Jeuteau also taught Clyde to play chess. It was over these games that Clyde learned much of his conversational French. It was a wonderful day when Clyde discovered that he could understand what was being said. The Ritcheys were ready for God to usher them into the next phase of their adventure.

71

ARRIVAL IN AFRICA

After graduating from their language studies in the fall of 1956, the Ritcheys packed, and made their way to Bordeaux where they boarded a French ocean liner. While on board Clyde had the opportunity to preach in French. This was good practice for him.

Field chairman Gordon Timyan met them in Abidjan, Ivory Coast. They stayed overnight at a hotel and the next day collected their baggage from customs and proceeded inland by train. When the train stopped at Dimbokro they met fellow missionaries Joe and Louise Ost who were waiting at the station to greet them. Joe and Clyde would work together on many building projects in the years to come. The train continued up through the middle of the country, on to Bouake *(boo-ah'-kay)*, the place that would be home to the Ritcheys at various times throughout the years.

Living conditions were better than anticipated. Clyde and Doris had expected to live in a mud hut with very primitive conditions such as they had seen in pictures shown by missionaries. Although the living conditions may have been considered primitive by some back home, the Ritcheys were pleasantly surprised to find that they would live in a house with a real roof—corrugated tin, of course—and not a grass thatched roof!

The walls of the small house were thick mud walls, but in the traditional rectangular shape they were accustomed to. Small animals, reptiles, and insects could be heard scurrying on the mat ceilings stretched high overhead. There were no glass panes in the windows, only loosely attached screens. The back door hung askew, a problem that Clyde soon repaired. Gauze netting was hung over the beds to protect the sleepers from mosquitoes. Running water in the house was supplied by water hauled by bucket from the very deep wells on the station. Water for each house was hauled to a water tower where it was pumped (by a Jappy pump) up to a barrel on top of the house. The storage barrels were not large, so everyone was frugal with the water. Bath water was prepared with water heated on the stove and poured into a large galvanized tub.

During those first days, Brenda came down with malaria and a high fever, and Clyde laid hands on her and prayed for her. The fever broke within fifteen minutes and she quickly recovered. The laying on of hands and praying in faith in God was a common practice in a day when medicine and medical help was not readily available

An electric generator housed in a small storage building supplied a few hours of electricity each night—enough to light one wavering light bulb in each of the mission houses. Kerosene lanterns were used to supplement the faulty lighting. The Ritcheys had a small kerosene-run refrigerator that had to be frequently defrosted. Drinking water had to be filtered, and the children drank reconstituted powdered skim milk. When it was discovered that Clyde was mechanically inclined, he was assigned to maintenance of station vehicles and the electric plant. Each night it was his responsibility to turn the electricity for the station on and off.

Once again the Ritcheys found themselves in a bewildering world as far as language was concerned. The Ritcheys' small house had a detached storeroom, which doubled as a study. Mrs. Janis Timyan conducted their language lessons in the storeroom. They wrote their own dictionary as they learned new words. Africans were invited to come to the house to visit with the Ritcheys, conversing in Baoule *(bah'-oo-lee)* so they could increase their vocabulary.

They attended church in Bouake where a Baoule service was held. After the monotonous chanting in the French services, Clyde and Doris were delighted to hear the beautiful four-part harmony of the Baoule voices enthusiastically lifted in song. They may not have understood the words, but many of the hymn tunes were familiar and the conviction of the singers was unmistakable.

There were plenty of adjustments to be made, but the Ritcheys felt at home in this new place to which God had called them—and God was once again proving Himself faithful.

FIRST TRIP INTO THE BUSH

In early October 1956, after having spent only a week and a half on the mission station in Bouake, the Timyans took the Ritchey family on their first trip back into the African bush, to an area near Beoumi *(bay-oh'-mee)*. The word "bush" aptly described an area that had scarcely been touched by civilization as known by that time. Of course, everything is quite modern today, but back then, going in to the bush was a step back in time to a culture that had changed little over the centuries.

After leaving the hard, rutted dirt road, which was characteristic of most roads in French West Africa, they started down a rough bush trail that led to several villages. After traveling a couple of miles, they could see where patches of the jungle had been cleared away and in their place were rows of coffee trees, banana plants, and yam patches. Finally, beyond these patches of cultivated land appeared their first glimpse of an African bush village. The road (such as it was) that led to the village quickly filled with children yelling and pointing. To see a car was a rare thing to them. Those who lived close to the road or were anywhere nearby stopped what they were doing to stare and point at these strangers.

The African lifestyle was as it had been for hundreds of years. Round huts were made of mud bricks with grass-thatched roofs. Racks of corn were strung in the courtyards to dry in the sun. The outside family kitchen was usually a shelter composed of a few posts covered with a thatched roof as protection from the sun and rain. Tobacco was hung in these kitchens to cure by the smoke from the kitchen fires. Old women could be seen sitting on the ground picking seeds out of cotton while others spun the cotton into heavy thread, as had been done for centuries.

Most of the children wore little or no clothing. Men wore shorts and sometimes undershirts, while the old men of the village were generally wrapped in black and white hand woven blankets. These elders would sit under a large shade tree, discussing problems of the village and settling palavers. At that time women generally wore no clothing from the waist up, with a long cloth wrapped around their lower body, and tucked in at the waist.

The missionaries arrived at the village where they were to conduct a one-week short term Bible school for men. There were at least 20 men between the ages of 18 and 40 who met each day for Bible classes. For the most part, their knowledge of reading and writing was limited, but, oh, the fire that burned in their souls! These men were natural-born preachers. When they stood before a crowd with a Bible in their hands, there wasn't any stammering and stuttering. They presented a clear-cut message of God's redeeming grace. The zeal and passion expressed by these men for their own people impressed Clyde. He could not help but contrast their response to Christ to that of Christians he knew in the States.

One thing that stood out in the services was listening to the Baoules sing such songs as *Amazing Grace, Leaning on the Everlasting Arms, There is Power in the Blood,* and *When the Roll is Called Up Yonder* in their own language. One could tell that these men knew first-hand what it meant to be saved! Their songs were more than lip service to God—they were a sacrifice of praise to the One who sent His Son Jesus into the world to save sinners, regardless of race or color.

Clyde was delighted to find that he was able to help some of the young men learn to read. Even though he had not yet learned the language, he discovered that Baoule was a language easy to read phonetically. Even he could make himself understood by reading the written word. This process also helped him to learn a few words.

In the meantime, Doris was introduced to another aspect of missionary work as she watched her children play with the little African children. She closed her eyes and silently committed Brenda and Mary Kaye to the Lord in prayer as they played in the same sand pile as a little child with leprosy. She could not offend the Africans by not letting her children play with their children. This was just the first lesson in learning to release their children into God's care— something that Clyde and Doris would have to do many times throughout their missionary career.

Brother Timyan asked Clyde to preach in French one Sunday, while he translated into Baoule for those who did not understand. The Bible school students accompanying them wanted to go to the neighboring village to advertise the meeting, so Gordon, Clyde, and a carload of lay preachers climbed into Gordon's truck and drove to the village. Upon arrival the young men led the group to the chief's house. As was the custom they went through the long ritual of greetings. Finally they told the chief that they had come to bring to him and the people of his village the message of the living God. The chief agreed to the meeting and sat down outside his hut where a large group of people had gathered from all parts of the village.

After a few words of introduction and explanation, one by one the lay preachers began preaching. They told of the fear and superstition with which they had once been bound in their fetish worship. They told of their vain sacrifice and their empty hearts. They told of how Christ, God's Son, came as a living sacrifice to redeem all men from their sin. They said they were not preaching a white man's religion, but a message for all men everywhere. Brother Timyan brought the service to a close by giving an invitation to those who wanted to accept Jesus Christ as their Savior. A sound of assent went up as he asked the crowd if they believed that what these men were saying was true.

It was on this occasion that Clyde saw the first heathen bow his knee upon African soil and accept Jesus Christ as his Savior. He was greatly moved as he observed that when the man finished praying, his first concern was for his brother who was standing nearby. This boy had a fetish bracelet above his elbow and a fetish ring on his finger. At the beckoning of his brother he came and knelt at his side as Clyde imagined Simon Peter had done at the call of his brother Andrew. There in the gloom of the African twilight, this boy too gave his heart to Jesus Christ. Without being told, the fetish ring was stripped from his finger and an attempt was made at removing the metal bracelet, but it was too small to pass over his elbow. The preachers left the village that night with the boy's promise that the bracelet would be cut off the next day.

On Sunday night a similar service was conducted at the close of the Bible school in the village where they were staying. With the aid of a car battery, slides of the life of Christ were shown and more singing filled the balance of the evening. Those who wanted to accept Christ were asked at the close of the service to go to a small church building on the outskirts of the village. Upon their arrival at the church Clyde and Gordon found the place packed to capacity. God was faithful and they saw more black brothers born into the Kingdom of God. What rejoicing there was among the believers of the village that night!

What an introduction Clyde had to the ministry

before him in the Ivory Coast! He was filled with great zeal and enthusiasm to share God's Word as he witnessed so many eager hearts, waiting to accept Christ as their Savior. But he was also saddened by the overwhelming lack of workers. Clyde wrote home, "It's marvelous to see the working of God's Spirit among these people. We feel sorry for missionaries who labor among other tribes in Africa and in other parts of the earth who see little or no result from their ministry. The thing that breaks our hearts is that we have so few missionaries (six couples in all) to labor among one million people who are responding to the message of Christ and salvation. Unless the church in America wakes up to its responsibility and opportunities and sends more missionaries, it will be the same story as in many other places: too much work with too little help—'too little, too late.'"

AFRICAN POWER ENCOUNTER

There was a Bible school on the Bouake mission station where young men were taught the Bible and preaching skills. It soon became Clyde's responsibility to drive these young Bible school students out to the bush on Sunday afternoons and drop them off at different villages to witness and preach. At the last village, Clyde would preach in French while an interpreter translated the message into Baoule. Then he would make the return trip to Bouake, picking up the young preachers at each place they had been dropped off. On these trips Clyde had opportunity to converse with the Bible school students, getting to know them and building his vocabulary. This exposure was invaluable, as these young men were to become the pastors Clyde would work with in the years to come.

Returning to Bouake from the village rounds one Sunday afternoon two of the students asked if Clyde would come with them to a nearby village. When they reached the village they explained there was a demon-possessed woman there who wanted to be delivered. Clyde wasn't sure the students knew what they were talking about. He asked, "How do you know she is demon possessed?" They told him the woman's story.

The woman came from a village three kilometers away—a village wholly given over to the worship of demons. As a small child, this woman had been presented into the hands of the witchdoctor of her village to be dedicated to demons for their habitation and use. This custom is much like the Christian's custom of dedicating a child to God. As the children reached puberty, the demons took control of their bodies, driving them out into the bush where they were used physically to fulfill men's sexual desires. The young person would come back to the village in a daze, torn and bleeding from violent encounters. This kind of life was all that this woman had known. When she heard these young men preaching about Christ and deliverance, she expressed her desire to be set free from these demons and demonic practices. Uncertain of how to proceed, the young men decided to wait until Clyde came.

Except for her eyes she looked like any other 20-year old woman. Her eyes were very dark—as if one could see the pits of hell in their depths. Full of compassion for the woman, but hindered because of the language, Clyde said, "All right, I'll pray for her. But I can't pray in Baoule because I don't yet speak Baoule, and it's no use to pray in French because she doesn't understand any French. I'll pray in English. That's my native tongue, and the God who hears in Baoule also hears in my language."

Clyde took the woman by the hand, lifted his eyes toward heaven, and uttered three words, "Oh, Lord

Jesus . . . ." At those words the woman fell to the ground as though hit by a fist. Her hand was torn from Clyde's, and she began convulsing on the ground. Clyde continued to pray, commanding the demons to leave in the name of Jesus Christ. Screams tore from the woman's throat until she finally lay quietly on the ground. When there were no more manifestations of demons the students helped the woman stand. The people gathered around, amazed by what they had seen.

Clyde said to the villagers, "Now I am going back to my village Bouake. But I will return; I want to be certain that she is completely delivered." The men left the village with the promise to return.

They were unable to return when planned, because Gordon Timyan, who was to accompany them, had been bitten by a snake one dark night the week before and was still recovering. It wasn't until the following week that they were able to return. When they arrived at the village, they discovered that the woman wasn't there. While runners went to the next village to get her, the villagers gathered for a service. Some of the elders of the church in Bouake had also come, and with the young preachers, they gave their testimonies. Gordon preached and then Clyde preached through an interpreter.

At the invitation, an old man stepped forward. He said, "I saw two weeks ago that the power of God was stronger than the power of the spirit I have served all my life and I want to repent and serve this God."

With him came 13 old men who entered his hut to kneel and pray one by one, accepting Christ as their Savior. Before the missionaries left that night, the 14 old men had burned their fetishes.

The woman was brought in after they had finished praying. When asked how she was, she responded positively. "Never in my life have I been filled with such freedom. But once in awhile I experience something like lights flashing inside my head." Gordon felt that Clyde should pray again for the woman. Clyde deferred to Gordon, as he could pray in Baoule so the woman could understand what was going on. But Gordon said, "No, you began this in English, you can finish it in English." The woman knelt at the bench where, shortly before, the old men had knelt to pray. As prayer went up the last demon finally manifested itself. The woman fell back on the ground. At the command the demon left with a scream, and the young woman was set free.

Several weeks later, on the steps of the church in Bouake, Clyde met the old man wearing a rumpled suit. The man asked Clyde, "Do you remember me?" Clyde said, "Yes, your face is familiar." "Well, take my picture, white man," the old man responded. "Show the people in America what a witchdoctor looks like after he is converted." That was when Clyde found out that the old man had been a witchdoctor. Now he understood why all those old men had come with him to accept Christ. They had all been part of a secret fetish society—keepers of the fetish.

About twenty years later, in December of 1979, the Ritcheys were asked to go to a nearby village to serve communion. The appointment didn't work out because the church had scheduled communion for another day, so they decided to move on to a small village not far from there, which was seldom visited by missionaries.

While they were singing the first song, a feeble and crippled old man haltingly walked into the church with the aid of a cane and took a seat at the front, as was the custom for the church elders. Clyde noted that for a very old man he was quite vigorous and had a booming singing voice. While watching the man sitting there with his cane grasped between his two shaking hands, Clyde leaned over and whispered to Doris, "That man looks familiar."

Before he got up to preach Clyde asked, "Old man, what's your name?" He responded, "Abraham." (This was his Christian name.) Clyde asked Abraham how he was saved. Abraham shakily stood to his full height and began to tell a long story of how, many years ago, a strange white man had come into his village. There had been a demon-possessed woman who had been delivered. Joy welled up in Clyde's breast and he was moved, as he heard Abraham give the testimony of how he had witnessed and experienced the power of the living God that was greater than that of the fetish he had served for so many years.

When Abraham concluded his story, Clyde went

up to him and said, "Old man, I was that young missionary." Abraham's eyes lit up and he threw his arms around Clyde. Then he called a young man who was sitting nearby and introduced him. "This is the son of the woman you cast demons out of that day. She lives in Abidjan now, but is still delivered and following Jesus." Everyone joined in the excitement. Others in the church also remembered the event. The old man's native name was Toto Kouadio *(koo-ah'-jo)*. The Ritcheys' hearts rejoiced. God had arranged for them to be in the church that day in the little town of Grogro, worshipping God with this brother who had come to Christ all those many years ago.

Sowing in the morning, sowing seeds of kindness,
Sowing in the noontide and the dewy eve;
Waiting for the harvest, and the time of reaping,
We shall come rejoicing, bringing in the sheaves.

THE MOVE TO M'BAHIAKRO

After completing ten months of language study the Ritcheys were asked to fill in at the M'Bahiakro *(mmm-bah'-eeah-kro)* station while Archie and Jeanette Powell were on furlough. The M'Bahiakro district was a difficult area of ministry. In fact, there was an area in the M'Bahiakro district that was very resistant to the gospel. Ngban was deeply steeped in animism. Later, when other missionaries ministered in the area there was finally a breakthrough when King Yao Luku, ruler of the Ngban area, expressed an interest in Christ and asked for an audience with the missionary. The king said, "I've been thinking about becoming a Christian and I'd planned to do it about Independence Day (August 7), but God has been speaking to me and I can no longer wait. I must come when God calls, not at my own convenience." That morning he prayed to receive Christ and took the Christian name of David. King David continued to rule the area after his conversion and by 1966 there were about 500 Christians scattered throughout 18 villages in the Ngban area.

However, it was before all this took place that Clyde and Doris visited in this area with an African helper by the name of Noé *(no'-ay)*. They held meetings in a village, and before they left they went to the village chief to "ask for the road" as was the custom. There was an exchange of gifts. Doris gave the chief some towels, and he gave the Ritcheys a chicken. As they were leaving a family called to them to come over to their place. They said they had been listening to the Word all week and now they were ready to repent and ask Jesus to be their Savior. The entire family knelt and received Christ as Lord.

Two weeks later Clyde received word that the man of the family had come down with spinal meningitis and was in the hospital in M'Bahiakro. Clyde found the man in bed, and suffering much pain as he faced eternity. As Clyde looked into his face, he wondered, "Does this man really understand the decision he made? Does he really know that Jesus Christ is his Savior?" He had to ask the man these questions. "Old man," he began, "this may be the last chance you have to make things right with the Lord. Did you really put your trust in Him that day? And if you die, whose hand is going to hold yours?" Through much pain and difficulty, the old man responded, "I'll never turn from Jesus. He is my Life." A day or two later the old man died. At the funeral service back in his village, many people heard the testimony of how this man knew who was holding on to him, even in death.

On a trip into the Ando area, Clyde brought his whole family and David, a Christian worker and interpreter, along with enough provisions for a week. Driving carefully down the hard dirt-packed roads, they were nearly wiped out by a native bus barreling towards them in the middle of the road. Clyde sharply turned the wheel of his Studebaker truck toward an embankment and got out of the way just as the bus whipped past them, tearing off the back bumper of his truck.

After all the excitement was over, they got back on the road and continued on their way, driving as far as they could into the bush. From there African runners packed their bedding and supplies on their shoulders and heads, carrying them several miles through the bush to the village. Young Brenda and Mary Kaye were carried on the backs of some of the Africans. When they arrived in the village the Ritcheys were shown to a small African mud hut they would share with an African family, which would be their home for the week of ministry. After a few days Mary Kaye and Brenda took refuge in the hut, refusing to come out. Their light coloring and smooth hair was such an oddity to the black Africans that everyone wanted to touch them. They soon grew tired of being a novelty and hid.

The response of these people in the Ando area was much different from the response in the Ngban area. People came forward at each altar call, praying and confessing sin. In spite of the M'Bahiakro area being a difficult area in which to work, the responses of groups such as these in the Ando area were an encouragement to the Ritcheys as they went about the Lord's work. Each soul that entered the kingdom of God was a miracle of new birth.

When not at work spreading the gospel in the district, Clyde and Doris studied Baoule at home with their language helper, Paul Yoma. Paul was born in 1916, and had been saved in 1936. He had worked with missionaries during the war years, and was no stranger to persecution for his faith.

One day when Clyde and Doris were studying Baoule with Paul they were interrupted by Paul's wife calling for him from the path to their house, which was about a hundred yards away from the mission house. She said something about a baby being sick. Clyde immediately left with Paul to see what was the problem.

Some of Paul's relatives had come from a bush village to visit him, and their one-year old child was not well. When Clyde and Paul arrived they found the mother crying with the child seemingly lifeless in her arms. Immediately the Africans began to pour water on the child to revive her. Clyde stopped them and told them to wrap the child in a blanket while he ran to get the truck to take her to the small native hospital in M'Bahiakro. As Paul Yoma got into the truck with the child, Clyde looked at the child and thought she was dead. They immediately prayed for the child and upon arrival at the hospital the child had rallied.

They went directly to the native doctor's office with the child. The doctor pulled down the child's eyelid and saw that the tissue was as white as snow. The palms of her hands were also white. The doctor said the parents had waited too long and that he had absolutely no hope for the child for she had acute anemia. However, he agreed with Clyde when he said that God was able and gave them a prescription for shots. They took the child home and went to work to save her life. Clyde and Paul laid hands upon her and prayed, asking God to spare her life. With their prayers they also acted. Clyde read in his medical book that drinking beef blood was good for anemia. In addition to the beef blood they also gave the child medicinal yeast three times a day, along with the shots that the doctor had prescribed. Within three days veins began to appear under the girl's eyelids. A week later, the child that the doctor had said could not live was sitting up, laughing and full of life. Certainly, the medicine had helped—and the food—but to God and to Him alone belonged the glory for the life of this child.

In spite of his joy at seeing the miraculous recovery of the child, Clyde was saddened by the thought that every hour of the day there were thousands in Africa slipping out into eternity with diseases such as this, of whom many had never heard the name of Jesus. They knew nothing of His saving power, let alone His healing power. Clyde realized he had not seen many lame or crippled people in Africa. As was true in many places in the world, the law of survival of the fittest reigned in this uncivilized land. Also, often those who were handicapped in any way were considered expendable when it came time to offer a blood sacrifice to satisfy the selfish demands of the fetish spirits.

One day shortly after the girl was healed Clyde prepared to cut a bunch of bananas from a banana grove to hang in the garage to ripen. He found a stalk that was mature, grabbed hold of its stem, cut it loose, and brought it out in the open. There were some dead leaves down among the bananas. Clyde started to pick them out with his free hand when all of a sudden he noticed something strange circled about the stalk. It didn't take him long to figure out what it was. He hurriedly set the bananas on the ground and called for the yardman. With one sweep of his razor sharp machete, the snake was dead. The yardman examined the snake and informed Clyde that the snake was of a deadly poisonous variety. Clyde was thankful that the God of Daniel was with him to shut the serpent's mouth.

As Clyde reflected on these and other occasions that God had shown Himself to be with him, he took comfort in knowing that God's Word had proven true in at least three points of His commission to His followers. Clyde had laid hands on the sick and seen them recover; he had cast out demons in Jesus' name; and now he had handled a serpent and it had not hurt him. As he reflected further, he could have added that he now spoke with a new tongue, although it came about through much study and hard work! However, without God's help he could never have come as far as he had. He was thankful once again that he served the true and the living God, a God who never sleeps nor slumbers, a God who always takes care of His own. Clyde affirmed to himself once more that he wouldn't belong to the Devil and his crowd again for all the riches of this earth.

MO SARAH'S ANSWER TO PRAYER

There was a godly old Baoule woman from Bouake named Mo Sarah, who would come to M'Bahiakro to visit with Paul Yoma's family. Mo Sarah's background was challenging, to say the least. She had accepted Jesus as her Savior as a young wife. When she became ill, her pagan husband kept urging her to sacrifice a sheep to the spirits who had become angry when she quit worshipping them. Finally she gave in and offered a sheep, entreating the spirits to leave her alone. Instead, one of them took control of her body and mind, and she became like a wild animal, wandering the bush and fields eating whatever she could find. She was chased from one village to another. Her hair became matted and her skin caked with mud. She was one of the "crazy" ones, or in the words of the Baoule, her "head was spoiled."

One evening she was lying in the grass near her hometown when she had a vision of two roads going in two different directions. A man dressed in white stood between the roads. He asked Mo Sarah, "Who can tell me where these two roads lead?" She looked and saw one was a broad road filled with many people and the other road was a narrow road and only a few walked on it. She knew the answer, for she remembered hearing about two roads in her church.

She answered, "The broad road is the fetish road which leads to death and the narrow way is the Jesus road which leads to eternal life."

The man in white then said, "Why don't you take the right road? Go back to your church and have them pray for you." She answered, "No, no, I can never do that as I have turned my back on Jesus and I have insulted Him!"

The vision was gone but the memory of the vision remained with her, urging her to return and ask the church people to pray for her. At first she fought every thought of doing so, but soon something inside seemed to loosen. She got up, went into town, and sought out one of the church elders. He gladly went with her to the little altar in the village church where they knelt to pray. He cried out for the Lord Jesus to have pity on Mo Sarah and heal her. She wept and wept because of the horrible sin she had committed against her loving Lord. For three days the tears flowed continually. She could neither eat nor sleep. Then suddenly the burden lifted and she was restored once more to fellowship with Jesus and His people. The Christian villagers rejoiced with her as her mind was completely restored and her body healed. Now everywhere she went she told of God's wonderful love and forgiveness to her and pled with others to walk on His road.

Mo Sarah stood out among the Baoule people. Everyone knew Mo Sarah. They knew that she was a woman of prayer. She could be seen walking down

95

the road, stopping dead in her tracks to lift her face toward heaven. Her lips moved as she motioned with her hands. Mo Sarah would touch heaven with her prayers anytime, anywhere. God was so real to her that by only a slight inclination of her head she would be instantly in His presence.

One missionary observed that many times while talking with Mo Sarah, she would include God in the conversation. When she died at the age of 102, this deeply loved and respected woman who had no birth children of her own had hundreds and hundreds of spiritual children to her account. People from all over the Baoule nation came to her funeral.

The Ritcheys were still in language study at M'Bahiakro when Mo Sarah would come to visit Paul Yoma. They did not yet understand everything that was being said in Baoule and Mo Sarah spoke no French. She would knock on their door, and when Doris answered, Mo Sarah would come in and motion to a chair in the living room. She would go to the chair, get down on her knees, and begin to pray. It wasn't until later that Clyde and Doris found out that Mo Sarah had been praying that they would have more children to give to the Lord.

Mo Sarah's prayers were answered. It was during this year that Doris found she was expecting the Ritchey's third child. As the delivery date of the baby drew near Clyde drove his family to the Baptist hospital at Ferekessedougou *(farah-kay-say-doo-goo)*, where the Ritcheys were installed in one of the cottages prepared for expectant families. When it came time for the baby's delivery, the mother would go to the infirmary, and then return to the cottage with the newborn.

On December 25, 1957, while Doris was in labor, Clyde and their two small daughters sat in the Ritcheys' truck outside the infirmary waiting for word that the baby was born. Clyde just knew this one would be a boy. When they finally heard a baby's cries through the open windows of the infirmary, Clyde exclaimed, "That's my Christmas present!" He jumped out of the truck and hurried to the window of the infirmary. There he was informed that his son Jonathan Clyde Ritchey had arrived. About twenty years later Jon would visit this same hospital again—but that's another story!

MOVING AND MIRACLES

At the annual West African field conference in 1958, held in Kankan, Guinea, the Ritcheys were reassigned to return to Bouake where Clyde was given the responsibility of ministering in two large districts—Bouake and Tiebissou *(tee-eh'-bee-soo)*.

Clyde and Doris returned to M'Bahiakro to pack their bags for the move. Their responsibilities in their new area of work would be greater than ever. The work in any one district was staggering enough. They were thankful to God for consecrated laymen and national workers who were a tremendous help in assisting them.

Clyde visited the new Tiebissou district that was without a missionary at that time and found that many villages showed an interest in the gospel. In these early forays, Clyde saw a number of new converts come to Christ. While working in that district, word came to Clyde one day that there were those who wanted to repent in a village about 25 miles away. After closing the conference he was conducting, Clyde left for the village, taking with him a native catechist, Lazare Kouassi, who would later be ordained and serve as pastor of the Tiebissou church.

They stopped on their way at another village where there were a number of Christians to pick up a few to accompany them. Upon arrival at the village, a Christian who had suffered much persecution at the hands of the animists greeted Clyde and Lazare. Then they were greeted by the townspeople in typical African fashion. They were given places to sit, offered water to drink, followed by lengthy greetings. Men were just then coming in from the fields after the day's work, so the Christians waited until more had gathered before conducting a service.

People began to gather around, some squatting on the ground, others sitting on hand-hewn stools, while others milled about. Finally the Christians began to sing. After a few hymns, Lazare preached the Word of God. At the close of the service, he invited those who wished to repent to come and kneel before the rest of the villagers. The evening sky was blackening with heavy clouds, and a few drops of rain began to fall. Normally, the villagers would have run for shelter, but instead, 16 adults and nine children stepped forward and knelt on the muddy ground where they were led in the sinner's prayer.

By now, the rain was falling quite heavily. They entered one of the native huts and all of these new babes in Christ gathered around and listened hungrily to further instruction from the Word of God. Clyde rejoiced with those who had found Christ as Savior.

The wide open doors to the gospel as indicated by the responses of these people were taken as an invitation by the Ritcheys to work in the Tiebissou district. The following year they were appointed to move to the Tiebissou district and concentrate their efforts there.

While still living in Bouake, the Ritcheys discovered they were expecting their fourth child. The baby was due about the same time they would be moving to Tiebissou. There was a great deal to do in preparation for this move. About that same time, Clyde ended up flat on his back with a bad case of hepatitis. He could not even move without being nauseated. When Doris went into labor, Clyde was unable to take her to the hospital. Fellow missionary Joe Ost drove her to the local native infirmary.

This was an anxious time for Joe since he and his wife Louise had never had children. As they went over each bump on the rough dirt roads he asked, "Are you all right, Doris?" Between contractions Doris laughed and encouraged Joe. An African midwife delivered Judith (Judy) Joy Ritchey on June 6, 1959.

Two weeks after Judy was born—with Clyde still sick and unable to help—Doris packed up the household and moved them all to Tiebissou. Imagine packing up and moving a whole household with a sick husband and four young children to care for—one of them a newborn! With Joe Ost driving the loaded mission truck, Doris drove the family in their truck to their new home. The first order of business was to unpack sheets to make up the bed for Clyde so he could lie down.

By then, Clyde began to feel that the illness was an attack from the enemy to hinder him from engaging in the spreading of the gospel. When word spread that the white missionary had arrived, Africans began to come around to ask when he was going to preach in their villages. Then the Ritcheys heard that Pastor Lazare was also in the local hospital, sick with tuberculosis, and not expected to live. It was clear that the enemy was getting in some heavy blows to prevent them from doing any further work in this new area. Nevertheless, they trusted the Lord for healing.

About two weeks after arriving at Tiebissou, Clyde woke Doris up in the middle of the night and declared, "The Lord has healed me." For six weeks he had been flat on his back with hepatitis—now all the symptoms were instantly gone. He had no more nausea or tenderness in his abdomen. In fact, he felt quite strong.

The next morning, Clyde got up, ate a good breakfast for the first time in six weeks, and then put in a concrete block wall around a 20-foot deep well that he was afraid one of the children would fall into. With the help of the yardman, he began laying block. It was hot and Clyde was perspiring, but he rejoiced as he felt stronger with each passing moment.

About that time Rev. Walter Arnold, the field director, drove onto the station from Bouake. Horrified at the sight of Clyde working so hard in the hot African sun, he asked, "What on earth are you doing?

You're supposed to be in bed!" Clyde responded, "I'm building a wall." "But you're supposed to be resting. You've got to be careful with hepatitis. You could easily have a relapse and end up worse than before." But Clyde insisted, "The Lord has healed me." He added, "Now we need to go down and pray for healing for Lazare who is in the hospital with tuberculosis."

The two men went to the hospital and prayed, asking God to heal Lazare. By the end of the week the hospital had released Lazare, completely and miraculously healed.

These miracles were confirmation to Clyde and Lazare that God was about to do great things in this district. With the men finally able to devote their attention to the work in the Tiebissou district, they found a field ripe for harvest. Through their faithful labors, many souls were brought out of the kingdom of darkness into the kingdom of God's marvelous Light.

A MOVING OF GOD'S SPIRIT

The year 1959 began with a group of believers from one of the churches in the Tiebissou district going on an evangelistic visit to one of the neighboring villages. The Word was preached and 20 new converts were added to the church of Christ. This was the beginning of what was to become a real moving of God's Spirit in this district.

Not long after the Ritcheys' arrival at Tiebissou in June, one of the local lay Christians stood up in church and testified that he wanted to be used of God in the salvation of souls. Moise *(mo-ease')* wasn't of the Baoule race. He had come to Ivory Coast from Nigeria in 1952. He spoke Baoule fluently and went from town to town on his bicycle selling various household products to the village people. His consuming desire and prayer was to take Christ wherever he went, and he became a faithful witness in town after town.

One Sunday he told Clyde, "Pastor, there is a large town about 35 kilometers from here that wants you to come and preach the Word of God to them." This was a surprise to Clyde and Lazare as they didn't know of any Christians at all in the vast area to which Moise referred. In fact, in the past the people of that area had been indifferent to the message of

Christ. They prayed together and started out over the rough bush road to the village. At last, after passing village after village, they arrived at a large market town called Koliankro and found a large group of people awaiting their arrival. There they preached the message of the cross and waited for the reaction of the people. What rejoicing there was as 21 people stepped forward and knelt in rows behind one another to pray the sinner's prayer!

On the trip back to Tiebissou, Clyde got stuck in the mud a little distance from another village. The townspeople came out to assist him and it was discovered that Moise had also witnessed in their village. When the people in the village learned of the conversions in the neighboring village of Koliankro, they insisted Clyde and Lazare come to preach in their village. A large crowd of villagers gathered to hear the gospel preached. At the close of the service a young man who spoke good French approached Clyde. He had been a soldier in France and while there had joined a Catholic church. Since returning to his home village he had gone back into fetish worship. He wanted to know the difference between Christianity and Catholicism. After an explanation, he expressed a desire to ask Jesus Christ to forgive him for his burden of sin. He knelt with five others and prayed.

This was the beginning of 55 conversions in that village in just a few months. Moise had done his job well, and it was with sorrow that Clyde learned soon after that Moise was the husband of two wives. He called Moise aside after a service one Sunday morning and confronted him with this accusation. Moise didn't deny it but went on to say, "When I came from Nigeria, I was a very weak Christian and didn't know the truths of God's Word as I have heard here. It was in this state that I took my second wife." Clyde asked him what he thought about it now. Moise answered, "I am living in sin, for now I know God's Word. I should have only one wife."

Sadly, he had a child by his second wife who would suffer because of his sin. Clyde told Moise he couldn't use him further in the work of God until he gave up this wife. Without hesitation Moise responded, "I have sinned. Pray for me. From this day forward this woman will only be a sister to me. I want to do the will and work of my Lord." He fell on his face before God and poured out his heart, asking for forgiveness. The joy of the Lord continued to be the experience of Moise and it was largely because of his faithful witness and fervent teaching that the numbers of believers in the villages he visited continued to grow.

During this time, God was working all over the district. People heard of the moving of God's Spirit and walked for miles to hear this message for themselves. One Sunday morning a delegation of six from a new village showed up at the service at Tiebissou. They prayed after hearing the Word. Another Sunday a group of 11 were brought to Tiebissou from a village

10 kilometers away by a lone Christian woman. They too prayed after the service. Word came for the missionary to go in another direction for people in another village wanted to hear the Word. Upon arrival they found a group of 13 who had not been able to wait, but had already prayed with a church elder from a neighboring village.

The Spirit of God was indeed at work. Nine new villages opened up in the Tiebissou district within the first year with over 200 conversions. This number did not include those who were being saved at the same time in already established churches. Unfortunately, only 30 believers were to be baptized as there was only one active catechist—Lazare—to do any teaching and preparing of new Christians for this act of faith.

A large church was built in Tiebissou for the growing congregation. This was the beginning of many fruitful years of labor in Tiebissou. Satan had tried to stop the work in the beginning, but God had won the victory. The challenge was greater than ever, but God was going before, building His church. Clyde prayed that more laborers would be sent forth into this needy area and that more consecrated lay preachers such as Moise would be raised up to continue the work that had begun.

Bringing in the sheaves, bringing in the sheaves,
We shall come rejoicing, bringing in the sheaves.

SIGNS AND WONDERS

During the years Clyde served in the Tiebissou district he saw many other instances of God's powerful hand at work. The Baoules were a very responsive people, and every time the gospel was preached people responded. People were not only being saved, but God was also doing unusual things in people's lives.

Clyde was called to the hospital in Tiebissou to take a dying Christian man home to a nearby village. The man had spinal meningitis and was very near death. If the man died in the hospital his body would have to be taken back to the village by ambulance, which would cost a great deal for the family. Pastor Lazare and Clyde went to the hospital where they found the man alive, but as stiff as a board. They put the man in the car and headed for his village. The people of the village knew he was coming.

As Clyde drove into the village the people were all gathered, crying and wailing, "He's dying! He's dying!" Caught up in the emotion of the moment, the man soon joined the cry, "I'm dying! I'm dying!" The man was carried into his hut where he was laid out on a mat on the floor. As Clyde stood there in the dark hut, he felt the Lord telling him to pray for the man. He turned to Lazare and said, "This man doesn't have to die. Let's pray." They laid hands on the man and prayed for his healing. Before Clyde left, he told the man that he would be healed. Two weeks later Clyde returned to the village and saw the man walking down the road with a hoe on his shoulder. God had honored His word and had healed the man.

God's solutions to our circumstances are not always the same. On another occasion Jacob, a young man who truly loved the Lord, fell sick. Clyde went out to the village and found Jacob lying on his mat, delirious. He went to the village chief and asked permission to take Jacob to a hospital to be treated.

After discussing the matter with the chief, permission was given. In the hospital Jacob seemed to improve a great deal. His family was with him to tend to his needs since medical care generally consisted of someone rushing in now and then to give medication or a shot. His family slept on the floor beside him to tend to him and provide his meals. Jacob seemed to be recovering nicely when Clyde had to leave for Bouake. Clyde and Doris promised the family that they would return later that evening to see Jacob. They were in Bouake only a short time when a taxi pulled up to the station with a messenger who urged them, "Come back to Tiebissou; Jacob has died."

Clyde was very troubled by the news. Jacob had been growing so wonderfully in the Lord. There had seemed to be such promise in the young man for the

Lord's work—and he had seemed to be recovering from his illness.

Clyde arrived back at Tiebissou where he would pick up Jacob's body to take it back to his village. At the hospital he asked, "What happened? He seemed to be getting along so well." The story was related that after the Ritcheys had left, Jacob had indicated that he wanted to sing a song. He took the Baoule hymnbook, opened it, and began to sing, "There's not a friend like the lowly Jesus, no not one! No, not one!" He sang all the verses of the hymn, closed the book, shut his eyes, and died.

For Jacob, to live was Christ, but to die was gain—now he was with Christ, the One he loved. What a change in the life of one who had once worshiped spirits and had lived in fear of displeasing them! Now Jacob was truly set free—not only from the hellish bonds that had once bound him, but now also from the physical bonds that had separated him from his Redeemer. Whether by life or by death, his desire was to glorify God.

During the Ritcheys' second term they also served a year at the children's school as house parents as well as having oversight of the Beoumi district. A single missionary nurse, Alice Ryan, and her father, a "retired" missionary occupied the Beoumi station. On one of his trips to Beoumi, Clyde put a roof on a school building on the station. That evening he prepared to hook the building up to the station's power plant. Old Mr. Ryan asked Clyde, "Why not hook up my house, too, as long as you are doing wiring?" Clyde asked, "Do you have a ladder?" "Sure, I've got a ladder."

While Mr. Ryan went to get a ladder Clyde looked over the situation. In order to hook up the wiring to the missionary house, Clyde would have to cut the wires that led into town. Electricity for the station had previously come from the town of Beoumi, but the town no longer had a diesel electrical plant.

Clyde set the ladder up against the 15-foot electrical pole, but the ladder was too short to reach the top. He would have to shimmy up the pole the rest of the way. Near the top of the ladder he cut the wire within reach. The pole gave a shudder. Ignoring the warning, Clyde shinnied up the rest of the way. At the top he straddled a thin guide wire that was attached to a tree some distance away. He reached up as high as he could to reach the remaining electrical wire. As he cut the wire the pole began to fall. The cut wire had been the only thing holding up the pole.

As Clyde began to fall face forward, he thought to himself, "When the pole gets close to the ground I'm going to throw myself off the pole." But he forgot about the remaining guide wire. As the pole began to fall away from the guide wire—toward the direction of the wire that had been cut—the guide wire snapped. Clyde was flung to the hard-packed ground as if he had been shot from a slingshot. He hit the ground hard on his back and bounced, hitting the ground hard a second time.

As he fell, Clyde yelled, "Here I come!" The yell brought people running from every direction. Paul Yao, the godly old African pastor, came running from his house. Doris and Alice came running from the mission house. Some of the African workers made a move to pick Clyde up, but Alice, a nurse, warned them, "Don't touch him until we see if he can get up by himself."

Clyde carefully put his hands on the ground and tried to lift his torso. He couldn't move. It felt as though his back was shattered. He exclaimed, "I can't move. This pain—it's terrible!" Paul Yao and Mr. Ryan, those two dear old men of God, knelt at Clyde's side, laid hands on him, and began to pray. When they had finished praying they said, "Now see if you can move." Clyde felt no change, but went ahead and put his hands down on the hard ground once more and began to push. To his amazement he was able to sit up. He was assisted to his feet where he found he could put weight on his left leg, but not the right.

With help he made his way to the Ryans' house where he ate a little supper. He was still in a great deal of pain and didn't feel like eating very much. He was then assisted to the old mission house where he and Doris were staying and made preparations to go to bed.

As all this was taking place, the Lord gave him a promise, "As they went they were [healed]" (Luke 17:14-16). God had already begun the work of healing, and Clyde could only trust Him to complete the healing of whatever damage had been done to his back and right leg.

That night Clyde carefully tossed and turned, moving slowly, trying to find a position that didn't hurt. Finally, he fell into a deep sleep. When he awoke in the morning, he gingerly moved his legs. He felt no pain. He slipped his left leg over the side of the bed, carefully putting weight on it. Then he carefully put his right leg over the edge of the bed and put weight on it. This was the leg that had hurt so badly the night before. He was able to put weight on both legs. There was only a little pain remaining in his back. He carefully made his way to the bathroom where he shaved and prepared himself for the day. He then directed the remaining work from a chaise lounge set up outside. By the end of the day he could walk without a limp and without any pain whatsoever—he was wholly and completely healed. As he went he was healed—as God had promised. Once again God had proven faithful to His promise to His servant—for His glory and praise.

GROWING UP RITCHEY—IN AFRICA!

(This section is written in the first person because it deals with personal experiences in my growing up years. ~ Brenda)

My earliest memories are from the year we were in France. I remember my playmate Danny, and some of the things we had done. I remember getting sick from eating cherries that had fallen to the ground in the back yard of the apartment where we lived, and once we climbed on his father's vehicle and removed the windshield wipers. My next memory is of being on the ocean liner heading to Africa from France. Mom and Dad put us in the ship's nursery when they went to the dining room for dinner, and I remember admiring the small child-size sink and toilet in the nursery's bathroom. I remember thinking, "How cute!"

As a little girl, I used to follow Dad everywhere and loved to watch him while he worked. He was always doing such interesting things. This practice got me in trouble at least once. One evening while we were living at M'Bahiakro, Dad left the house to shut things down for the night. He headed for the hen house, not realizing I was following. Hearing something, he swung the lantern around and severely burned my arm with the hot glass. That painful

113

event didn't stop me following him around, however!

One time while traveling back to M'Bahiakro from Bouake in an open Jeep, Dad had to make an emergency stop by the side of the road. He hurriedly pulled the car off the road and leapt out of the Jeep, not realizing that Mary Kaye had been leaning against him. She tumbled out the door after him and rolled down the embankment. There was no harm done, it was just another adventure.

While Mom and Dad were still in language study in Bouake, Mary Kaye and I were napping in our bedroom when Mom discovered a snake crawling along the wall near the ceiling. She called in a yardman who quickly dispatched it. Another time when we were playing in the open-air building known as "The Tabernacle," Mom heard us screaming, "Snake! Snake!" Mom came running to see a snake wriggling along the floor. She picked up one of the benches stacked along the outside walls, turned it upside down on top of the snake and stood on it until one of the Africans came along and killed it.

As our parents had done before us, we found our entertainment from the things around us. I wasn't as interested in playing with cars as I was in making roads and villages around the fantastically intricate tree root systems, creating gardens, and making little houses. We also enjoyed climbing trees, especially the large mimosa in the middle of the Bouake mission compound, or picking frangipani (plumeria) flowers and breaking the long slender thorns off the crown of thorn plants that circled the compound in order to see the white sticky sap ooze out. Of particular interest was touching the tiny leaves of the "touch-me-not" plant and watching the leaves fold up against the stem. Some of the things we learned to watch for were sitting down where there were ants that gave painful stings; and avoiding playing with the pretty orange and red chili peppers, which if handled could even hours later give a painful burn if rubbed in the eyes.

We had no television or video games, no telephones or shopping malls. We spent time learning from our parents, playing with puzzles and games, reading good books, playing with our toys, making houses with blankets draped over furniture, baking cookies or other goodies, playing in the sandbox or on the swing set and so much more. These were just ordinary activities to us—extraordinary when you consider what children do today to fill their time. Judy remembers, "Our entertainment was reading. How I loved reading good books and laughing a lot." We were content with these simple things. We were encouraged to exercise our creativity, as well. I learned to paint by doing paint-by-number sets. I used to make dollhouses for my little sister Judy from cardboard boxes, with steps going up to a second floor, furniture with matchboxes glued together for a chest of drawers, a bed made with scraps from Mom's sewing box, wallpaper on the walls, etc. Judy says that these houses were better and prettier than any she's seen since. I also used to make doll clothes from Mom's sewing scraps, sewing the tiny clothes by hand.

My brothers freely roamed the jungles and countryside around our compound, bringing home birds, lizards, or snakes shot with slingshots, BB guns, or pellet guns. In that day there was no fear of kidnappings, molestation, or racial hatred such as there is today. Looking back, it really does seem as though it was a time of carefree innocence.

In the 1950s and 1960s, the only beef available at the big, noisy open-air markets was from cattle that had been driven down from Mali or Burkina Faso. By the time it reached our markets it was usually tough and stringy. It hung in the open stalls with flies buzzing around it as portions were sliced off for customers. Mom would have to pressure cook it to tenderize it. As a result, most of our meat came from a more plentiful source—the deer, horse antelope, and wild pig Dad and my brothers brought home from their hunting trips. We also enjoyed eating the large-mouth bass, known as "capitan" caught in the rivers near our town.

Speaking of food, another memory I have of home is of churning homemade ice cream. This is a tradition Dad brought from his growing up years. We girls started the churning, adding ice and salt as needed. As the churning got harder, the boys would take their turns and Dad would finish. After the ice cream was churned, Dad would pour the salted ice water at the base of two coconut palms we had growing in our front yard. I'm not sure if it did any good. I guess he figured that since coconut palms grew near the ocean, salted water couldn't hurt them.

Dad also tried to raise bees. My sister Judy remembers that the first time she saw Mom wrapping Dad's legs and arms with bandages she thought he'd gotten stung and Mom was "fixing" him. This was actually part of his "bee gear." He also had a hat with netting that loosely protected his head and shoulders. He was quite a sight in his "bee gear," holding a smoking funnel can in his heavily gloved hands. I don't ever remember getting any honey from those hives—African bees are not heavy producers of honey—although Judy does. She says the honey was the best she has ever eaten—probably because Dad had to work so hard to get it. I do remember, though, sitting at the dining room table one day, painting, when I heard a loud droning sound getting closer and closer. Looking out the window, I saw a black funnel of bees flying into a new hive Dad had just built. It was sitting on our back porch until Dad had a chance to put it out on a distant corner of our property. He found the chance pretty quickly after that—dressed in his bee gear, of course.

As his dad did before him, Dad raised chickens— and sometimes turkeys and ducks, as well. Dad kept them dusted for lice and inoculated them against disease. They roamed our compound during the day and went into their large pen and henhouse at night.

When we'd hear them cackling loudly at night Dad would take off with his gun to see what critter was bothering them. We had a plentiful source of eggs and chicken. There was one big old rooster that used to chase us, terrorizing us while we were hanging clothes out to dry. We were thankful when that old guy finally made it into the cooking pot!

On one occasion, Dad kept a watchful eye on a fully-grown hen with a tumor on her chest. The tumor was quite large, and Dad thought it best to isolate this hen from the other chickens. He put it in the garage pit with food and water, and shortly after that we went away on vacation, forgetting all about the hen. When we got back, while unloading the car, he heard a sound from the pit. Walking over, he peered over the edge, and saw a small chicken walking around. The food was gone, and the hen had fasted for some days, which had shrunk the tumor. She had survived on her own body fat, greatly reducing her size. He was quite chagrined that he had forgotten about her. She was restored to her family and soon regained her size. The tumor never came back.

We would wake up in the mornings to Dad playing the radio, listening to ELWA ("Eternal Love Winning Africa"), The Armed Forces, or Voice of America (VOA).

Our days began and ended with family devotions, reading from God's Word and praying. We all participated. Many times as children, we witnessed Dad in his office in the early morning hours while it was still dark outside, reading his Bible by the dim desk light and praying. These observances made an impression on all of us children.

One of the most difficult sacrifices missionaries make is in parting from loved ones. The first painful parting takes place when they leave for the field or for language study. This sacrifice is repeated at the end of each furlough, and is more bittersweet with each goodbye as loved ones grow older and more dear, and with it the knowledge that this might be the last time they would see some of these loved ones ever again in this world. But even more difficult than these partings were the partings with their children as they were sent away to boarding school to live under someone else's care.

I was the first of the Ritchey children to go away to school. Mom spent hours making new clothes, sewing in nametags, and then packing up my trunk with all things I'd need for the next eight months. The school at Mamou, Guinea was a three-day journey by car over bumpy roads and over or through rivers. There were frequent stops to repair tires and engines, for picnic lunches, and for bathroom breaks. Although my parents had tried to prepare me for leaving home, the reality hit after we had traveled down the road a distance. I was six years old, and the only way I had to describe my homesickness was to tell the wife of the man driving, "My tummy feels funny."

I do not have many memories of Mamou. I do,

however, remember admiring the flowers and bushes growing around the dorm. The pretty white jack-in-the pulpit flowers growing out from the nest of dark green leaves were of particular interest to me. I remember the swimming pool, the dark hallways in the dorm, having to wear slippers at night on the way down the hall to the bathroom because of the scorpions that would gather around the small lanterns on the floor that provided light. I remember eating white rice with cinnamon sugar and milk for breakfast. I went to Mamou for first and third grade. Second grade was in the States while on furlough.

In 1962, the Conservative Baptists opened a new missionary children's school in Bouake, Ivory Coast, which was, of course, much closer for us. We saw our parents more often, and had more breaks to go home than at Mamou. It was at this school that Mom and Dad would serve on three separate occasions as dorm parents, five years in all. ICA (then Ivory Coast Academy, later called International Children's Academy) had been good for their children and they were glad to do their part in supporting its on-going ministry to other families in this way.

We children were proud that other kids got to see how wonderful our parents were. Our mom was a great cook, and impressed the grade school boys with her homemade pizza and cinnamon rolls. She was also usually willing to fry up their "catches" of small fish and other small game from their forays into the countryside. But she really wowed them when she hit a homerun in their softball game. Dad always had a following as he repaired cars, made things in the shop, or took time to discuss matters of importance. He had a way of giving several viewpoints and providing the child the opportunity to form his or her own opinion.

Going away to school was as difficult for us children as it was for our parents. But Mom and Dad had taught us early in life about priorities and making the most of the time we had together. Our parents always played up the positive side: how much fun we would have making new friends and playing with old friends; enjoying special activities—and after all, it was only so many months before we would be reunited—and in the meantime there would be visits, weekends at home, and weekly letters.

Mary Kaye and I were at boarding school at ICA when our youngest brother Danny was born on November 18, 1962. Several years later, when I was 13 or 14, Dr. Dwight Slater told me about Danny's birth while trying to put me at ease during our annual physical examinations at school. He said, "I'll never forget when your little brother Danny was born! He was delivered early in the morning, and that same day your mother invited our whole family over to the cottage for supper. She made a big meal including Southern fried chicken and homemade biscuits for our large family." Still impressed, he declared, "That woman was born to have babies!"

As the eldest, I was often charged with watching

out for my baby brother. I carried him around every-where and loved mothering him. When we were away at school, Mom learned to become suspicious after long periods of silence. One time she smelled smoke while sewing in her bedroom. Getting up to investigate she followed the smell to the boys' room, where she discovered Danny's bedspread on fire. She quickly bundled up the bedspread and threw it out the back door. Looking for Danny, she found him hiding under the bed he had set on fire!

Tiebissou was "home" for us for most of our grow-ing up years. Since Tiebissou was on the main route between Abidjan and Bouake we received many vis-itors. Mom was well known for her hospitality and cooking. No matter what she had cooked for her fam-ily of seven, there was always a way to make it spread out for company. Mary Kaye and I were used to being ousted from bed in the middle of the night so Mom could remake the beds with clean sheets for the visitors. We didn't mind a bit! We loved "camping" on the large screened-in front porch with the exotic sounds of the African night lulling us back to sleep. I can still hear the eerie tree lemur's night song, be-ginning with a soft, low "Ha. Ha. Ha. Ha," escalating in sound, tempo, and pitch culminating in an eerie screech that lifted the hair on the back of one's neck. We took a kind of shivering delight in the scariness of it, knowing we were safe.

Another sound I loved was the sound of rain on a tin roof. Even today I love a full-blown thunderstorm, with lightning flashing and thunder rumbling through the northeast Georgia foothills. I'm sure this is due to the magnificent displays I witnessed as a child of the tropical storms during the rainy season. They were at times quite violent with flashing lightning and explosive claps of thunder. The sound of pounding rain magnified as it hit the tin roof overhead. Rain would collect on already oversaturated ground, forming pools of water, running off in streams as it sought lower ground. I can remember my sister, Mary Kaye, crying one day, at about age 9, as she watched the red rivers of muddy water flowing past the house. She was afraid the world would be destroyed as it had been in the days of Noah, or as Pompeii and Herculaneum had been destroyed by a volcano. We were prolific readers by that time, and she had just finished reading "The Last Days of Pompeii," which had made her aware of the potentially destructive forces of nature.

Dad enjoyed planting and tending fruit trees. We had a pineapple and banana patch, different kinds of mango trees, orange trees, grapefruit trees, and lemon and lime trees. We also had a couple of coconut trees, papaya trees, guava bushes, and avocado trees. At times we had so much fruit we loaded down our departing visitors with the excess. I'm sure the African yardman and our neighbors enjoyed their share as well.

Dad's storeroom was famous. He was a packrat as far as his workshop was concerned. It was filled with every motor, engine, and appliance we had ever owned—stored until some useful part might be needed. A visitor with a car problem might find his engine repaired with a washing machine part. There were times when we were on the road that I remember him fixing our car with wire, string, or bubble gum, so that it at least limped along to the next town. He was quite ingenious with his solutions. Dad was skilled in many areas, self-prescribed as "Jack of all trades, master of none." He would say, "If I can't fix it, it can't be fixed; and how do I know until I try?" He figured that if someone else could fix it, so could he. He made most of the furniture in our house as well as some of our playthings. His creative engineering also gave us one of the first hot water systems in the Ivory Coast. Visitors passing through in those early days marveled at being able to take a hot shower. The system became more elaborate until a real hot water heater eventually replaced it.

One day, Dad made plans to be out in the bush preaching for about a week. He left me—a young teenager at the time—with the responsibility of lighting the hot water system each night. He showed me how to fill the tank with kerosene and light the pilot light. Upon his return he went out that first evening to light the pilot light. He opened the fuel area, gave one sniff, and bellowed my name. When I appeared, he asked where I had been getting the fuel for the heater. I showed him the container and he just shook his head. I had run out of kerosene the night before and had used gasoline from the container next to it. He took me back to the heating system, threw a lighted match into the general vicinity of the pilot light, and we watched in silence as the entire area burst into flames. Shaking his head, he said, "Your guardian angel must have been working overtime to prevent you from being severely burned."

One morning in 1961, while preparing to go to the States for furlough, with the car sold and household packed up, my little sister Judy came down with a high fever at the breakfast table. She began to convulse. Since we had no vehicle, Dad quickly wrapped her up in a blanket and began to run up the road about a quarter of a mile to the hospital. While he was running he was praying. About half way there he stopped and realized that she was not breathing. Her face was white. He laid her on the ground and prayed that God would have mercy on him and not allow her to die. As he held her, a large gasp of air flew from her mouth. Dad said he believed God spared her life, because she began to get better from that moment on.

On another occasion Danny had gotten a shot for yellow fever. It was from a horse serum that it turned out he was allergic to. He developed a high fever and convulsed several times. In the hospital, the doctor gave him something to counteract it and told us that Danny was never to have anything again with horse serum, or it would kill him. He recovered, but I remember many times after that whenever he got sick,

Danny would beg, "Pray for me, Daddy!" He had faith in Daddy's prayers, and had a strong dislike of swallowing pills.

Besides his bush ministry, holding evangelistic meetings, and other ministries, Dad also frequently preached Sunday mornings in the church he had built in Tiebissou, taking turns with Pastor Lazare. Mom would sit near the back of the church with us five children. We were not always quiet and good, as I'm sure Mom longed for us to be. I can remember occasions when Dad would interrupt his preaching in French to say in English, "You kids had better settle down NOW, or you will be getting spankings when we get home. Think about it." Then he would continue his sermon, as if there'd been no interruption. We thought about it and listened.

There were usually plenty of diversions in church. One of the church elders would patrol the aisles with a long pole that served a dual purpose. When time for collecting gifts and tithes, he would slide the end with a cloth pouch down the aisles for people to put their money in. Other times, he would patrol the aisles, using the other end to nudge people who fell asleep in church. The recipient of this rude awakening often received some good-natured ribbing from those in their vicinity.

Speaking of spankings, as children we were well loved and when we were punished, it was because we had earned it. As a four-year-old, I can remember being warned about walking outside while barefoot, since we could easily pick up parasites and worms from the African soil. I remember well what followed when Dad caught me outside after defying such a warning—the same ritual that always had the power to bring me to tears long before I ever received the spanking. He would place me on his knee, look me in the eye and start talking. "Now Brenda, do you remember when I told you not to go barefoot? Do you remember why? Your Mommy and I don't want you to get sick, so to remind you not to do this again, I'm going to have to give you a spanking. This is for your good, and it's going to hurt me much more than it will hurt you." That was the gist of it, but it was usually much longer—and more painful than the spanking.

Mom usually deferred to Dad for punishment, but she could step up to the plate when necessary. I remember getting my mouth washed out with soap once for sassing my mother. Actually I was a fairly placid and obedient child and didn't get punished a lot, which is why Mom says I can't remember getting many spankings.

Dad's practice was to not mete out punishment right away as his father had done, but to wait until he had cooled off—which gave us some time to think about what we had done and think about what was to come. One time he spanked my youngest brother Danny while still angry, and felt so badly about it that he couldn't sleep that night. Finally, he got up and awoke Danny to tell him, "Danny, I'm sorry I spanked you while I was angry. I should have waited until I had cooled off." Danny just rolled over and said, "That's okay, Daddy, I 'owed' it."

Dad frequently spent the day, or several days, in the bush on ministry, often coming home with interesting stories. In the early days of his ministry, an angry fetish chief threatened him. This took place in one of the first villages that had responded to the gospel in the Tiebissou area where a Christian had his teeth knocked out by the hostile chief of the area. Later another Christian came in to Tiebissou bleeding, with his shirt torn. He reported that the chief and his men had taken all his cocoa and coffee harvest and dumped it in the forest. The chief was doing all the damage he could to get rid of the Christians in his village. Since the government guaranteed freedom of religion for all people, Dad went to the gendarmes (police) to report the incidents.

When the gendarmes heard Dad's story they said, "Let's go!" The gendarmes filled one truck and Dad picked up a couple of Christians to take along in his truck. They all drove out to the village. When they got there everyone in the village came out. The old chief of the village looked at Dad and said, "White man, some day, I'm going to tie you and beat you to death, because you're the one who brought division into this village. Before you came we were all one. We all worshipped the fetish and were content. And now these Christians have come. They break our worship days, spoiling our ground, and spoiling our water." The fetishers worshipped the spirits on Wednesdays and Sundays, much as Christians honor the Lord on Sundays, except the fetishers kept the entire day of Wednesday as a holy day, while the Christians worked on this day.

The gendarmes warned the chief, "If you beat any more of these Christians you are going to go to jail." And that is where the chief eventually wound up—in jail. Yet, in spite of all the persecution in that village, the church grew rapidly, which proves the old saying, "The blood of the martyrs is the seed of the church."

Because of stories of such threats, as a youngster, I became worried when Dad didn't come home one night when expected. When he finally arrived home, he inquired, "What in the world are you still doing up so late?" "I was worried, Daddy. I thought you were dead." He explained, "Brenda, I'm only spending my time on earth doing the Lord's work. When His work for me is done, THEN He will call me home. And when that happens, you can be sorry for yourself, because you'll miss me—but don't be sorry for me. I will be where I want to be—with the One for whom I live and serve." Because of our parent's teaching, we learned that death was not a thing to be feared. What a change this was from the young boy from Portage who grew up afraid to die lest he end up in hell. Dad knew in Whom he believed and served, and he had the assurance that one day he would be face to face with his beloved Savior. Until then, he had work to do.

It was in such a way that we children developed the belief system we have today, from the experiences, discussions, and devotional times we shared at home. My late pastor's wife was fond of quoting, "In part I was born. In part I was made. In part I make myself." We were born into a loving family, and the experiences to which we were exposed helped us to make the decisions that made us who we are today.

ANGEL OF THE AIRWAVES

For about two decades, seven nights a week, Radio *(rah-day-oh)* Evangelique *(ay-van-gel-leek')* CMA *(say em ah)* was on the air. This daily half-hour program in Baoule was beamed into the Ivory Coast from radio station ELWA in Monrovia, Liberia. In fact, ELWA's powerful transmitters reached far beyond the limits of Ivory Coast. Letters came from dispersed Baoule listeners in Ghana and Togo, and reports came from Upper Volta and Mali indicating that a clear reception came through to these far-off places.

How did this ministry come about? The missionaries noted that people were being born and others were dying faster than the missionary could ever hope to reach them. And, with the advent of modern progress, groups of people were being dispersed, forming new villages miles from the center of their own tribal groups. Always before the missionaries were the words, "This gospel of the kingdom must be preached in all the world, as a witness to all the nations, and then shall the end come!" (Matthew 24:14) This radio ministry began as a means of reaching those who were still waiting to hear the gospel message. The vision gave birth to reality as programs for radio began to be recorded.

Because Clyde was the only missionary at the

time with a cassette recorder, he was asked to join in this effort in the 1960s by preparing radio programs in the Baoule language. Radios were a rarity in those early days, and the possibility of radios becoming a common commodity in Africa was a dim hope. Yet the hope remained that somehow the radio messages would reach those areas unreached by the presence of the missionary or African layman. It was not long, however, before small transistor radios and large boom boxes could be seen in homes, carried around by young people, or listened to in the villages in the gathering places under large mango trees.

In the beginning, Clyde began preparing eight-minute messages for radio on a little hand-wound Butoba recorder, under the shelter of large cardboard cartons to deaden sound. In 1975, Clyde built and equipped a recording studio in Bouake with state-of-the-art equipment and began to produce quality recordings for broadcasting. Technological advances made it possible for even the poorest person in Africa to have a small mass-produced transistor radio. Hundreds of tapes were produced each year, sending the gospel messages over the airwaves.

There was a variety of programming. One very popular program was the Saturday night program, which featured Baba Andre *(ahn'-dray)*—Daddy Andrew and his children, a program aimed at youth. Another popular program was the Tuesday "Question and Answer" program, in which Pastor Aser *(ah-sair')* answered questions received from radio listeners.

These variety-type programs were interesting to all. But the backbone of the broadcasts was the Bible teaching and evangelistic programs. Letter after letter told of how the preaching of God's Word had brought conviction. Other listeners were challenged or built up in their faith. The Bible teaching ministry was not only important but essential to those who depended on this radio ministry for the only spiritual food they received. The Baoule pastors who brought the messages on these programs became enthusiastic as they saw the far-reaching results of their ministry.

A few bewildered listeners wrote that the people in Monrovia spoke good Baoule, not realizing that the programs did not originate from Liberia. These Baoule programs were made in the C&MA radio studio in Bouake, recorded on good quality cassettes, and mailed off to ELWA where they were transmitted back into the country. Programs were made several weeks in advance to allow for poor mail delivery, which confused some listeners who wrote questions for the Tuesday evening "Question and Answer" program, not understanding why their questions were not answered on the next broadcast!

These daily broadcasts were one of the very few programs in the Baoule language and Christians and pagans alike called it "their" program. Missionary Dave Arnold made a visit to a new village where he and a group of Christians asked permission to hold an outdoor evangelistic meeting that evening. After the usual exchange of greetings demanded by protocol, and the request being made to the village leaders, the chief said, "Yes, you can have a meeting, but you must wait awhile. It's almost time for our radio program. You can listen to that with us first." Dave said they would gladly wait, and that they had come with this same message.

The testimonies that came from this ministry were compelling confirmation that Christian radio was a viable means of evangelism. An African pastor from another mission came to Bouake for a meeting. His mission did not work directly with the Baoules because his work was with another language group. He told of whole villages of displaced Baoules out in the farm areas where large groups were meeting together, forming their own churches, fed and held together mostly because of the Baoule radio programs. The groups numbered from a few meeting together in a yard to groups of 30 or 60 or more. One group was over 100.

Pastor Etienne *(ay'-tee-en)* Yao came from a visit with friends and relatives in the Soubre *(soo'-bray)* area to record some messages for his Monday night Bible study program. He was all fired up because everywhere he went people knew him. "Oh yes, you're one of the pastors who speaks to us on the radio!" Wherever he found Baoules he discovered they were listening to the broadcasts. In his own district of Tiebissou there was a palaver (discussion) in one of the villages among the Christians about a moral issue. The local leaders came up with a solution, but in the end they decided, "We'll write Pastor Aser's 'Question and Answer' program and he will give the right answer!"

For Clyde, who would rather be out preaching, working for hours confined in a radio studio was not always easy. But overriding this task was the overwhelming joy of listening day after day to Spirit-filled men bringing forth the Word of God. Godly men such as Andre Kouadio would spend all morning recording one message after the other for about four hours straight through. Their sound doctrinal teaching would go out as daily spiritual food to the thousands of Baoule Christians who would otherwise struggle along with a minimum of teaching.

Many of the listeners sent letters asking pointed questions about marriage, native customs and the Christian, religious denominations, teaching on demons, women's place in the church, sports and the Christian, etc.

An offshoot of the radio ministry was the cassette ministry. Nearly 200 cassette players, each with a supply of tapes, were sent out into the various districts as a tool for evangelism and to help the overworked national pastors. These tapes and players were left in villages where there was no pastor. On one occasion Clyde went with an evangelist into a remote village in the Bouake district. While there, they picked up a player and tapes left with a blind man and his family. This man was asked some questions about the messages to which he had been listening and the answers came readily, showing that the tapes had been listened to over and over again. It was hard to measure the "success" or "results" of these ministries, but the Ritcheys felt that its value was beyond measure in results for the kingdom of God.

While Clyde worked with recording messages, Doris handled the correspondence and tract ministry. Doris wrote home to the States: "Radio is a mighty instrument to convey God's Word. You would be thoroughly convinced of that if you could read some of the many letters we receive. Daily Bible teaching over the air is enabling even pagans to write in intelligent questions about the Scriptures. Many write that they are ready to become Christian, and what do they do now? Others say they are afraid to accept Christ because of pressures from fetisher parents and fellow villagers. We are moved when letters come from Christians in isolated spots saying that our program is their only source of spiritual food and encouragement. Continue to pray for our daily Baoule program and the faithful Baoule pastors who help produce it." She added, "I can't stress enough how vital the radio ministry is, or account for the far-reaching effects of the gospel going over the airwaves a half hour night after night into cities, towns, and villages all over the Ivory Coast. It boggles the mind and rejoices the heart!"

This ministry that began with so few radios in the hands of a few people quickly became one of the most powerful tools for ministry among the Baoule people. Radio was one of the reasons for the rapid growth of the church and believers in Ivory Coast— from 25,000 believers in 1955 to over 300,000 believers when Clyde and Doris retired in 1991.

In July 1990, ELWA suffered from massive destruction during a civil war in Liberia. In 1992 the radio station was resurrected and was on the air until 1996 when it was once again silenced. It has once again been resurrected and its vision, initiative and management placed in the hands of the nationals.

The voice of Radio Evangelique CMA may be silent, but its fruit remains. "So shall my word be that goeth forth out of my mouth: it shall not return unto me void, but it shall accomplish that which I please, and it shall prosper in the thing whereto I sent it" (Isaiah 55:11).

Sowing in the sunshine, sowing in the shadows,
Fearing neither clouds nor winter's chilling breeze;
By and by the harvest, and the labor ended,
We shall come rejoicing, bringing in the sheaves.

HIPPO ATTACK!

During the summer of 1979, the Ritchey's middle child and oldest son Jon went out to Ivory Coast to visit his parents in Bouake. He was a 21-year old student at Toccoa Falls College at that time and had worked on dredges and tug boats in the Gulf of Mexico for a couple of summers in order to earn money for college—and to set aside a little for a trip back "home." His mother had written letters to the States telling of fishing trips where his dad and others had caught 30-50 pound capitan, or Nile perch, a fish similar to a large-mouth bass. In fact, his mother had caught one of the 50-pounders! With his friend Kelly Vickers in tow, Jon boarded the plane to Ivory Coast with his new fishing equipment packed, full of anticipation of catching the "Big One." They were joining Jon's sister Judy who had arrived from the States a few weeks earlier.

Clyde and Doris had saved their vacation time that year in order to spend it with their children, and Clyde planned to spend a lot of that time out on the lake with his son. On July 19, Jon, Clyde, and Ray Stombaugh (Clyde's cousin and also a missionary in Ivory Coast at that time) took off for a day of fishing, while their families and Kelly went to a nearby town where they spent the day swimming and playing tennis. By noon the fishermen had their ice chest nearly full of fish, 4-10 pounds each or more, with other larger fish tied alongside the boat. After eating lunch they decided to take one more lap around the lake before returning home. It was then that Jon hooked the "Big One"—a large Nile perch weighing between 40-50 pounds. It was quite a struggle to land the fish, but Jon was thrilled with his catch.

The boat was carefully guided around submerged logs and rotten waterlogged trees. Jon, thrilled with his catch, was seated in the front of the boat, with his feet propped up against the prow, when all of a sudden he gave a shout and disappeared. In the same instant the boat was overturned and Clyde and Ray were thrown out of the boat by the massive body of the hippo that had taken Jon under water.

Clyde emerged from the water and grabbed at a small tree that was about four inches in diameter. He looked around while standing in the submerged crotch of the tree. He saw Ray clinging to the overturned boat, but all that remained of Jon was the churning water where the hippo had gone down. Despair clutched at Clyde's breast as he thought his son dead. Under the water the hippo held Jon's right calf, piercing it through as he violently shook him back and forth. With his leg still in the jaws of the hippo, survival instincts kicked in as Jon lashed at the hippo with his free foot. The hippo released him and Jon shot to the surface. He was able to fill his lungs with air before the hippo firmly grasped Jon once more, this time piercing him in the upper thigh. Realizing that he could not escape this time, Jon experienced a deep calm and committed his soul to his Lord Jesus. "I give my life to you, Lord. I can't get out of this." Jon felt the hippo's mouth open and he was miraculously released from the hippo's grasp. To his amazement he shot to the surface once more, about 10 feet from his father.

Clyde saw Jon surface and shouted, "Jon, are you hurt?" Jon responded, "Dad, I'm hurt badly." Clyde saw the hippo surface about thirty feet beyond Jon. How did the hippo end up that far away from where Jon surfaced? God's hand was at work. The enraged hippo roared like a mad bull and lunged toward Jon once more. Holding on to the flimsy branch, Clyde yelled to Jon to swim toward him as fast as he could. Three times the hippo went under as he surged forward with his mouth wide open in his fixed course toward Jon. In spite of Jon's wounds he raced through the water toward his father. The hippo made roaring noises as he leaped out of the water toward his intended prey. Clyde clung to the small tree with his left hand and stretched out as far as he could toward Jon with his right hand. The hippo was right at Jon's heels when Jon's hand grasped Clyde's. Clyde yanked his son into his right arm as he precariously hung on to the tree with his left. At any moment he expected the momentum of the hippo's lunges to wipe them both out. Ray was seen striking blows toward the hippo with the broken fishing rod he still held in his hand.

The men called out to God for help. The very instant Jon reached the safety of his father's hand the hippo was again seen at least thirty feet away, looking back at them.

The hippo went down again, and Clyde again cried out to God, "God, send it away. Save us!" The hippo was next seen sixty yards away, then one hundred yards away. Turning his massive head, the hippo saw something they could not see, and could not get away fast enough.

The men were about sixty feet from shore. Their boat was overturned. They had lost everything that had been in their boat. Jon clung to his father's neck as a red haze covered his vision. He said, "Dad, I'm getting faint." Ray, who was holding on to the boat, called out to Clyde that he could see that Jon was bleeding badly from the wound on the backside of his right leg, just below the right buttock. Clyde reached around and put his hand into a deep hole about three inches in diameter, going straight into Jon's leg toward the pelvic bone. He hurriedly jerked at the large sweat-stained bandanna he'd been wearing all day, wadded it up, and thrust it deeply into the wound. After a few moments the bleeding stopped. The doctor later told Clyde that this action saved Jon's life. Clyde could also see a large hole that went all the way through Jon's lower leg just above the right ankle. Again, he precariously balanced himself on the small tree as he tied his spare bandanna around the upper part of Jon's leg to act as a tourniquet. During all of this time, Jon never lost consciousness. They found out later that he had lost at least four pints of blood.

Realizing the urgency of getting help for Jon, Ray tried repeatedly to turn over the heavy wooden boat, but he had no success. Finally, he was able to at least push the boat toward Jon and Clyde where they carefully laid Jon across the back of the boat. The strong current slowly pulled them toward the center of the lake while gasoline poured from the outboard motor, badly burning Clyde's stomach and chest as he pushed from the back of the boat.

After at least a half-hour of struggling against the current, the men decided to abandon the boat and swim to shore with Jon. This would require Jon's help since both men were exhausted by this time. Gritting his teeth, Jon valiantly swam between the two men while they supported him. They swam from limb to limb, branch to branch of the trees rising up from the lake. They finally neared the shoreline and were able to stand and drag Jon to shore. Exhausted from all their exertions, they carried him about twenty-five feet up a hippo wash where they all collapsed. There they took stock of the situation.

It was now about 3:30 in the afternoon. Jon had deep punctures in his right calf and thigh. He also had other cuts, bruises and abrasions around his abdomen where his body had been between the hippo's jaws. Ray and Clyde were in their fifties and physically spent, yet one of them had to go for help if Jon were to survive. He would bleed to death if he were carried any distance. Since Clyde had preached in this area many times in the past, he knew that there was a village about seven kilometers away where he could get help. Clyde left his son in his cousin's care and disappeared into the dense jungle undergrowth.

Ray tore his shirt into strips to bandage Jon's legs. He did his best to keep flies, ants, and other insects out of Jon's wounds while they waited for Clyde's return. But Jon hesitated, remembering some of his survival training. He knew that eggs of blowflies laid in the wounds would produce maggots that would keep the wounds clean. Ray talked to Jon to keep him from going into shock. As dusk settled around them, Ray began to be concerned about Clyde's welfare, as well as Jon's condition. Jon was now in terrible pain. To make matters worse, it was getting cold, and a strong wind was whipping up waves as it blew on shore. They had no clean water to drink, which Jon needed because of the loss of blood, and they didn't have any matches for a fire. Jon had lost his shoes and trousers in the water. Ray put his tennis shoes on Jon's feet, covered Jon's shoulders with his own wet trousers, and then lay next to him, rubbing him briskly, trying to get Jon warm. They lay there in the dark praying for Clyde's safety and their rescue. It would be nearly midnight before they heard Clyde's voice and knew help was on the way.

In the meantime, Clyde had made his way along

shore, tripping over roots and falling into deep troughs made by hippos. At last, about a hundred yards along the banks, he came upon a small trail that led through the tall elephant grass and found an open space with a large mango tree. He continued through the brush until he came on an old abandoned path that was familiar to him. In his relief at finding the path, and anxious to get to the village, he neglected to mark the place he came out of the bush.

In spite of his fatigue, Clyde made good time as he ran to the village. At the outskirts of the village he found a man working in the field. Customs dictate that long greetings take place. The man finally gave the long explanation of how things were with him, his family, etc., and finally asked, "How does it go with you?" With relief Clyde was finally able to share his story. The farmer immediately brightened and said there were two schoolteachers in town with mopeds that could help him. He volunteered to run ahead and alert the men. Clyde requested that when they come they bring a blanket because Jon had lost all his clothes and they had nothing to carry him on. He ran on ahead to the town while Clyde, dragging, came along more slowly. At the edge of the village, the two men on mopeds came out. Clyde climbed on the back of one of the mopeds.

Retracing his path, they could not find the small footpath Clyde had used earlier. The young men knew of another path and insisted this was the only one it could have been. They went beyond that and ended up at the lake. Going back they continued to search, to no avail, for the path Clyde had used. Having wasted a great deal of time, Clyde sat on a log, dead tired and discouraged, not knowing what to do. He wept as he thought of his son, perhaps in shock or dying. He thought of his cousin Ray who had health problems of his own. He knew they must wonder where he was. He wondered how he would tell his wife that their son was dead.

Returning to the village, Clyde sought for a way to get to the town of Tiebissou, thirty-five kilometers away, where there were missionaries and an African pastor he knew. As they sat in the darkness, a beautiful sound reached his ears, the sound of a truck approaching the town. "Oh God," he prayed, "if only that vehicle could take me to Tiebissou." The vehicle turned out to be an African taxi bringing people back from market in a neighboring village. As the truck drew near, it slowed, and the driver stuck his head out the window and exclaimed, "Why, Pastor Ritchey! What are you doing here?" The driver was someone he knew!

The driver unloaded his customers and their market goods and turned around to drive Clyde to Tiebissou, speeding as though on a paved highway. Clyde's head met the top of the vehicle with every bump on the mud road. As they neared Tiebissou he could see the streetlights where young people gathered to study. Recognizing some of the young men, they slowed their vehicle to request as many as could to gather flashlights and batteries and wait for him to return. Going on to the African pastor's house, he requested help since he had good transportation. The pastor sent him on to tell the missionaries what was going on while he went to get gas for his truck. It was now nine o'clock in the evening, over five hours since Clyde had left his son and cousin in the hippo wash.

Clyde was glad to get a good long drink of water at the home of the Rurrups who now lived in his old home at Tiebissou, his first drink since earlier that afternoon. Then Clyde asked Darren Rurrup to drive to Yamoussoukro to get help from anyone he knew who might have a boat, and drive around the lake to Clyde's car and get the car battery and his floodlight, which could be operated from the battery. He then drew a crude map of Jon and Ray's location on the lake and gave Darren the keys to his car. Clyde found out later that God had already prepared another missionary in Yamoussoukro who had his boat attached to his car ready for an early morning fishing trip. The two missionaries rushed out to the lake to get Clyde's car battery and searchlight from his car. This would be a perilous trip—a boat on Lake Kossou at night, with submerged trees and branches in the water, and hippos active at night. With the floodlight and hand drawn map they set off to locate the survivors.

Meanwhile, Clyde returned to the village where the villagers were amazed he had returned so quickly. He had left on a moped and returned by truck. They headed back to the river with some African trackers. In the truck they also carried blankets, water, and a folding cot to be used as a stretcher. The Africans accompanying him divided into two groups to look for the trail that would lead to the lake. Finally one of the trackers shouted out, and everyone converged in his direction. He shown his light on a bent leaf and noted, "Someone came this way about five hours earlier today." They began cutting a path with their machetes until they came to a clearing with a large mango tree. Clyde recognized it as the same large mango tree he had passed earlier that day. Full of joy, Clyde began to run ahead of the others, shouting as he went. Arriving at the shore they found an oar floating in the water and the water jug from the capsized boat. The tide that had prevented them from reaching shore earlier had turned, washing everything back to shore.

Meanwhile, back at the hippo wash, Ray was doing his best to keep Jon warm and protected from insects, except blowflies. By this time Ray was nearly naked, as he had covered Jon with his clothes. At one point he saw an African fisherman in a pirogue and jumped up to stand on the shore, waving his arms and shouting for help in various languages. The fisherman looked his way and instead of turning toward them, rowed away as quickly as possible. What he saw was a large naked white man, which he believed was a ground spirit, trying to lure him to shore to eat him.

As darkness fell, stark, bone-racking pain began to set in and Ray was aware that Jon could go into shock. Ray lay down beside Jon to keep him warm and prayed out loud for him as they waited for rescue. They discussed reasons why rescue had not yet arrived. The hours lengthened as they heard the hippos snorting out in the lake, coming up for their night feeding on shore. They prayed, "Lord, don't let a hippo come up into this wash; anywhere else, but not here!" And no hippos came up that well-used wash that night.

Clyde and the Africans with him were going along the shore, calling as they stumbled and waded through the muddy shoreline. Finally, Clyde stopped and said, "I'm going on ahead. Will anyone go with me?" The Africans hesitated. "You know there are a lot of hippos feeding along the shore tonight." But Clyde pushed ahead, rushing through the shallow water with a flashlight to light his way. He continued calling, but the night wind was blowing against him, not allowing his shouts to reach ahead to the survivors.

After about 300 yards of stumbling and falling in the dark Clyde heard Ray's voice calling "Over here, Clyde." Clyde called, "Ray, is Jon still alive?" It was with great relief he heard the answer, "Yes. He is still alive." Clyde would never forget the moment when he finally shone the flashlight down into the face of his son—still alive after nine hours of unbelievable suffering. Jon's smile shone bright as he saw his dad, but his eyes had sunk back in his head and pain etched lines in his face. Clyde dropped the flashlight and other things he carried with him, fell on his knees and wept as he embraced his son. He said, "Jon, I love you." Jon replied, "Dad, I love you, too." And Jon also began to weep, as for the first time in all those hours he finally knew he would be rescued. "I'm glad you made it, Dad. I had just about given up."

It wasn't until Clyde had covered Jon's body with blankets that Jon began to shake. He had fought off the pain and shock for so long that he finally gave in when help arrived. Clyde held his son in his arms until the shaking finally stopped. By then the missionaries with the boat had seen the flashlights and had come to shore. They put Jon on the cot and carried him by boat to the Rurrups' truck. Every hole they hit in the road on the trip was agonizing to Jon, but he only squeezed his father's hands harder and groaned at times. They were thankful for the paved roads when they arrived in Tiebissou.

With Clyde and Jon finally on their way, Ray and the other two missionaries went across the lake to Clyde's car. They held the spotlight out in front of the boat to avoid hitting stumps sticking up out of the water. The wind and the waves were strong and it took about three hours to get across the lake. From there Ray drove Clyde's car to his home in Toumodi, an hour's drive away, where he was finally able to tell the anxiously awaiting families what had occurred. Doris immediately packed their things and with Danny, Kelly, and Judy, drove to Bouake.

Clyde arrived in Bouake at about 3:00 in the morning. He was too exhausted to continue on to the mission hospital at Ferkessedougou, another three hours drive away. The field director Jesse Jespersen called the hospital to let them know they were coming while his wife Ann, a nurse, gave Jon a shot of Demerol to ease his pain—the first relief he had had in twelve hours of intense suffering.

Before they left to take Jon to Ferekesedougou, Joseph Koffi, the godly old man who was the national church president, a man who had seen Jon grow up alongside his own sons, laid his hands with great compassion upon Jon and prayed. "Oh God, I'm not asking You to heal him. I'm asking you to give him total restoration. Make him perfect as he was before."

Jess and Ann Jespersen then drove Jon to Ferekessedougou, the hospital where Jon had made his entrance into the world twenty-one years before. There, a team of three surgeons and nine nurses were already prepped for the surgeries of the day.

While Clyde slept, Doris and the family drove to Bouake to join him at about 6:00 in the morning. About two hours later they received a call from the hospital informing them that Jon was in surgery. As soon as the car was repacked they were on their way, with Kelly driving because Clyde was still exhausted by his long ordeal.

Over fifteen long hours had passed from the time
the hippo had attacked until the time Jon reached
the hospital. That early in the morning, they found
the hospital lit up. As soon as Jon arrived they delayed other surgeries to immediately attend to Jon's
wounds, working on him for four or five hours. God
had provided a visiting bone surgeon from the States,
in addition to the other highly skilled staff.

Jon received four pints of blood from various individuals throughout the day, the first from an
African nurse. Several hours were spent cleaning
maggots, ants, dirt, and other debris from Jon's
wounds. Dead muscle, ligaments, and tendons had
to be removed. The deep wounds had been exposed
to the elements for so long that they could not be su-
tured—they were cleaned and stuffed with gauze
soaked in Betadine to heal from the inside out. The
visiting surgeon informed Jon's parents, "Jon could
possibly lose his leg due to the very deep wounds in
his upper thigh. But we are going to do everything
we can to save his life. If everything goes the way we
feel it should, the very best prognosis is that Jon
would have a very bad limp the rest of his life because of all the tissue that was removed."

The days passed with Jon's fever going up, going
down, with continuing surgeries. In addition, it
turned out that Jon was allergic to the anesthesia, so
they had to do all the surgeries without anesthesia.
Over the next few weeks Jon went through four surgeries in addition to skin grafts. Clyde couldn't bear

to see his son in such pain, so he stood outside and prayed while Doris remained to hold her son's hand.

One bone was slightly chipped by a hippo's tooth, but no bones were broken. One muscle was badly damaged, although the doctors were optimistic that the other muscles around it would compensate for the damaged one when Jon began to use it again.

After six weeks, Jon was released from the hospital. During that time he had not taken a step. They returned to Bouake where Doris continued to tend to Jon's wounds. One day she called Clyde to look, and there was his son with a big smile on his face, standing in the doorway with a pair of crutches.

Jon and Clyde would discuss the fact that God had spared Jon as a part of a greater plan for his life. Jon was to later say, "On Lake Kossou I died. What remains of my life belongs to Christ." He completely surrendered his life to God. When he returned to college he changed his major from Elementary Education to World Missions.

In January, Jon was able to return to the States to finish his studies. He worked hard on his own form of therapy, running up and down the steep hill beside the Ritchey home in Toccoa. He was able to walk without a limp and even rejoined his college soccer team. He had experienced God's hand on his life in an awesome series of miracles. He had gone through extreme trauma and had survived. He would forever bear the scars on his body, but his life would also never be the same. From a quiet, shy boy, he became a man anointed by God for His work.

As God's hand may be seen over and over again in intervention throughout this story, one might wonder why He permitted the incident to occur in the first place. The answer is surely that He might show His glory. This story has been recounted by Clyde many times from pulpits and to groups all over the United States, and each time it has touched hearts, as indicated by those who respond to the invitation given at the end. The hearers never forget the challenge given by Clyde, "You are safer in the mouth of a hippopotamus in Africa when you are in the center of the will of God than you are on the streets of your hometown or any other place in the world out of the will of God." However, it was a long time before Clyde, Ray, or Jon felt like going fishing again.

As the Ritcheys reflected on all that had occurred, they could not help but feel that God had a purpose for their son's life. That observation was realized when, 10 years later, Jon and his wife set off for language study in France in preparation for serving God in Guinea, West Africa. They served in Guinea two terms before changing course to serve in South America where God has continued to use them.

THE BATTLE ENGAGED

Clyde and Doris's second daughter Mary Kaye once remarked that a vivid childhood memory she had was of her father daily praying on the armor of God in protection against the attack of the enemy. Clyde was ever aware of the unseen battle being waged in the heavenlies. Where God was at work, Satan was working harder.

And God was at work! In October 1981, evangelist Dr. Howard O. Jones held revival services in the cities of Bouake and Abidjan. Thirteen services were held with 2,000 to 3,000 in attendance at each service. Over 1,000 decisions were made for Christ.

Clyde held a weekly Wednesday night Bible study to help teach some of these new believers. The meetings were long because each of the new believers wanted to give his testimony. These Wednesday night meetings continued for many years. One young man who used to attend the prayer meetings met Clyde again after a few years. He reported that he had moved away to another village where he began sharing the things he had learned in the Bible study, especially the lessons in Corinthians, and during that time had led 60 people to the Lord! There was left a good group of Christians in that village because of this young man who shared his faith.

The Ritcheys were in a village church one Sunday morning sometime later when the church leader mentioned that this was the first Sunday morning since the beginning of the year that there had not been at least one person (often several) to accept Christ. There were 310 people present. This was an indication of the constant growth all the Baoule churches were experiencing. Evidences of God's blessing were on every hand and in every ministry.

The Ritcheys could not help but wonder how long such unprecedented freedom to spread the gospel would last. Such liberty to preach God's Word was unusual, and the response of the people was wonderful to see. Great—even mighty—things were happening among the Baoules. Opportunities to present the gospel were numerous and many individuals were coming to Christ. God was giving a harvest—but Satan was getting in a few blows as well.

In 1988, in one of Clyde's TEE (Theological Education by Extension) classes, one of the students, a teacher from a nearby village said, "Pastor, I have an unusual story I'd like to tell you." He proceeded to tell Clyde about a powerful witchdoctor, whose custom it was to go into a trance and call demonic spirits to consult with him. Usually at the end of three days the demonic counselors would be present and the witchdoctor would make his wishes known (for healing, wisdom, etc.). This time it didn't work. A few days later he tried again and after three days the spirits came. The witchdoctor asked, "Why didn't you

155

come when I called you the first time?" They responded, "We have been in conference, deciding on strategy because Jesus Christ is coming soon and we have much to do before that time." The witch doctor was bewildered. He asked the demons, "Is this Jesus stronger than you?" They replied, "Yes." The witch-doctor privately wondered, "Why am I serving these spirits when there is a Spirit more powerful than they are?" The man sought out a Christian from the village of Clyde's TEE student. The former witch doctor turned from his fetishes, and became a Christian.

Clyde wrote to a church in the States:

> "We are in a great spiritual conflict, the like of which we haven't seen in the last thirty-five years in the Ivory Coast. The devil knows his time is short, and has released his rage against us for the work we are doing for the Lord. We are dependent upon your prayers—and the prayers of all the saints in America—so that we will be able to stand firm and fight the good fight of faith for His glory and praise.

> "Here in Africa we have churches holding all-night prayer vigils because we experience first-hand the raw powers of darkness all around us. In America the enemy has been subtler, wooing individuals away from God and the necessity of the protection of prayer. But the enemy is just as real and ugly in America as he is in Africa, and if you haven't felt his blows yet, you soon will as this age

156

draws to an end.

"Even the Muslims put us to shame as we hear them send out their early morning call for prayer over our city. Wherever they are, thousands of Muslims join together in prayer. We must awaken our sleeping troops—the church of God—to the urgency of prayer. Then, instead of reporting on the invasions of Satan on God's kingdom, we will be making advances into Satan's kingdom."

The battle was engaged. That same year (1988) four Maranatha Bible School students came down by train from Bobo Dioulasso *(jew-lah'-so)* in Burkina Faso to Bouake for Easter weekend. Late at night, at the end of their break, three of the students, Georges, Antoine and Abel, boarded the train for the return trip to Bobo. They were in second class, with no lights in the train car. A short way into the trip, Georges felt something hit him high in his chest, then again on the other side. In a sudden flash of light he saw a hand with a knife raised high to strike again. He kicked out and knocked his assailant across the aisle.

The passengers the assailant fell upon thought he had lost his balance and pushed him away. He fell back toward where the boys were sitting. This time the assailant plunged his knife into Abel. He and Abel fell together into the aisle. Because it was dark, Antoine wondered what was going on. He got up quickly and found Abel on the floor. He asked what

157

was the matter. Abel said, "He killed me! He killed me!" Those were the last words he ever uttered. He had been struck in the heart and died almost immediately.

The man lunged at Antoine with his knife, but Antoine evaded him. The knife nicked a nearby 16-year-old boy in the neck. By this time the passengers realized what was going on. They overcame the attacker and killed him—swift African justice. The train officials called ahead to Katiola, the next town, to have an ambulance waiting. Antoine, Georges, Abel, and the wounded boy were brought back to the hospital in Bouake. Since the assailant was dead there was no way of knowing why he acted as he did. Antoine and Georges recovered and returned to the seminary. Later Clyde and Doris were privileged to go to Bobo to attend their graduation and to see these young men go out into the work for which they had prepared.

Clyde felt that the attack on these men was of the enemy. Along with the reports of God's blessing he also recognized that Satan was working hard, getting in as many blows as he could to slow the spreading of the gospel. But he also rejoiced, that "greater is He that is in you than he that is in the world!"

Another blow to the work occurred in October 1990. At that time Doris had been working with the Christian bookstore in Bouake when an audit and inventory revealed that the bookstore worker had been doctoring the accounts and stealing money. The audit showed that over the years he had taken over $10,000, with the stealing accelerating over the last six months. Doris worked closely with him and had become suspicious of his lifestyle. He was living a life of luxury compared to the salary he had been paid. When questioned, he told Doris on different occasions that his father was helping him.

When Doris found out that he had been stealing, she felt betrayed, for he was a likeable fellow and they had always gotten along well. As is typical of many sinners, he was sorry he got caught, but not sorry for what he had done. He needed a spirit of repentance before God could do anything to radically change his life.

In 1990, Clyde wrote in his Chairman's report:

> "Never in the history of this field have we been beaten about, knocked down, and sustained the casualties that we have this past year. At a time when we should have been increasing our missionary forces, we have suffered incredible losses. God saw fit to take the wives of two of our missionary families this past year through their untimely deaths. Two more of our missionary couples will not return to our field because of moral failure. One other couple has gone into a needed ministry in Canada for at least three years. Resistant malaria, hepatitis, and Epstein-Barr Syndrome have badly crippled the ministries of several of our missionary families. On the financial

side, the weakening of the American dollar has wrought havoc with our field commitments, badly curtailing ongoing and new ministries. The large deficit in the Great Commission fund had taken away our hope of building churches in key city and other projects that need year-end grants.

"The national church, our reason for being here, has also been under attack as it has never experienced before. Moral failure has destroyed the ministry of at least three of our most promising preacher boys. Financial disaster has struck our primary school system in ways that will take many months to unravel. Fraud, corruption, and just plain dishonesty have disrupted the operation of these schools and place them in grave jeopardy.

"But our testimony has been that of Paul's in 2 Corinthians 4:8-9. He too was troubled, perplexed, persecuted, and cast down. But we are not distressed, not in despair, not forsaken, and not destroyed. Yes, we have suffered casualties, but in all things we are more than conquerors. All of these adverse things and direct attacks of our adversary have caused both the mission and the church to draw up battle lines. We are not unaware of our resources in Christ Jesus. As a part of the body of Christ in Ivory Coast, we have determined to daily put on the whole armor of God so we stand firm in the midst of the conflict, 'and having done all, to stand.' There would be no opposition by the enemy if it weren't for the fact that God, too, is working as we have never seen before. God knows and the devil knows that time is running out. Let us look at God's work and how He is going to finish the work He has given us to do."

With all these blows, surely the church would reel. But God was not silent, nor inactive. Portable chapels set up in new areas were soon too small for the crowds that gathered. Two and three services were held each Sunday morning in Bouake with crowds of 500 to 1,000 gathering for each service. Large baptismal services were held, with 100, 200, or more being baptized each time.

Bible school students in summer ministries had powerful responses to their outreach assignments. One young man reported leading over 80 people to the Lord in just one month!

One month a layman from another district picked up tracts from the Christian bookstore in Bouake to distribute in his district. A month later he returned for more, saying that he had won over 120 people to the Lord in that time. Wherever the Word of God was spoken it brought a return. Satan may have won some battles, but God was and is winning the war.

The last few years of ministry on the field were spent in leadership as Clyde accepted the mantle of field directorship. This was not his first choice—he would rather be out in the bush preaching. But these were days well spent as he and Doris traveled around the field, spending time praying with and encouraging the missionaries who had been going through difficult days of loss, illness, and spiritual discouragement. One missionary told him he was ready to quit. Clyde asked him if he still had the barrels he had used to pack his outfit. The missionary said yes. Clyde then asked him in which barrel he would pack his calling. All these many years later, the man and his family are still serving God as missionaries.

As retirement drew near for fellow missionary, Joe Ost, he was invited to speak in a village that had never heard the gospel of Jesus Christ. He wrote of this experience: "As I drove over that jungle road for the first time, I was really surprised to see seven villages that I had never seen before. I was amazed! The rains had washed the atmosphere crystal clear. God's light in the firmament—a beautiful tropical moon—was filling the cloudless sky and covering the earth with its mellow, yellow light. Did you ever see an unevangelized Baoule village basking in the light of the tropical moon? Did you ever know of the holy anointing and feel the urge to stay and tell them the old, old story? I drove through these villages and felt the old exciting thrill and the urge to stay out here longer. But we realize we have to leave. I can go home and tell young people there is still a lifetime of challenge awaiting them in Ivory Coast."

This yearning to be in the work of the Lord never leaves His anointed, and this was Clyde's experience as he faced retirement. While continuing to preach in churches in his homeland, Clyde was ever conscious of the tragedy of the open door—too many hungry souls and not enough workers.

This story has been the record of the triumphs of spreading of the gospel and the tragedy of those who continue to die while still waiting to hear the gospel in the Ivory Coast.

Going forth with weeping, sowing for the Master,
Though the loss sustained our spirit often grieves;
When our weeping's over, He will bid us welcome,
We shall come rejoicing, bringing in the sheaves.

RETIREMENT

In December of 1991, Clyde and Doris came to the States for retirement after one last missionary tour to the churches. Before they retired, The Christian and Missionary Alliance commended them with a plaque recognizing nearly four decades of mission work. At the same time they received recognition from the government of Ivory Coast, upon recommendation by the church with whom they had worked for so many years. Clyde received the prestigious "Chevalier Merite Ivoirien" (Knight of the Order of Meritorious Service to Ivoirians), the highest recognition given to a civilian.

While their term of service in Ivory Coast was completed, they continued to share the burdens of the church in prayer and with others from pulpits all over the United States.

Fourteen years earlier, in 1977, they had put a down payment on a house in Toccoa, where they hoped to retire one day. Their two eldest daughters, Brenda and Mary Kaye, were employed locally, and would make house payments on the house while living in it, along with any of the younger children who would need housing while attending college. The house was paid off by the time the Ritcheys retired.

In 1997, extensive plans were made for renovations to the old house, which had been built in 1953. Old wiring and plumbing also needed to be replaced.

On December 11, fourteen days before Christmas, the Ritcheys found themselves standing outside on their driveway, shivering in the freezing night air as flames and smoke shot up through the roof of their house.

Earlier that evening the members of the Ritchey household had been occupied in normal activities in the home. Clyde, Doris, Mary Kaye and cousin Steve were watching news on TV when Brenda noticed a funny smell in her bedroom. Upon investigation, it was thought to be smoke, but no one could figure out what it was or where it came from. Brenda moved her project out to the dining room table where she continued wrapping Christmas gifts.

At about 6:30 p.m., the doorbell rang. Doris and Mary Kaye questioned whether it was the TV or the doorbell. Clyde got up and opened the front door. Oddly, no one was there. However, his eye was caught by a strange flickering of light reflecting off the car windows. He ran up the steps in front of the house to investigate. Turning around, he saw flames shooting up from the roof of the house. Running back down, he shouted, "The roof is on fire, call the fire department!" Brenda dialed 911 and informed the operator of the fire and location.

Most people wonder at some point what they would do in such a situation. Now the Ritcheys knew. Peter wrote: ". . . though now for a little while you may have had to suffer grief in all kinds of trials. These have come so that your faith—of greater worth than gold, which perishes even though refined by fire—may be proved genuine and may result in praise, glory and honor when Jesus Christ is revealed" (1 Peter 1:6-7, NIV).

In those seemingly endless moments, they stood together as a family watching the fire and smoke billowing from the roof of the house which had been home for over twenty years and they experienced perfect peace and trust in the One who provided them with all things. They were reminded of Jesus' words: "Do not store up for yourselves treasures on earth, where moth and rust destroy, and where thieves break in and steal. For where your treasure is, there your heart will be also" (Matthew 6:19-21, NIV).

A fireman later commented on how calm they were and asked why they hadn't tried to remove any valuables from their home. Clyde motioned to his family and replied, "The most important things are right here with me." Although there were personal items in the house, irreplaceable by this world's standards, they knew they had something more important. They had an eternal inheritance that can never be destroyed, kept in heaven (1 Peter 1:4).

It turned out that the fire began due to old electrical wiring in the attic, and most of the fire damage was confined to the attic and roof. The electrical engineer determined that the electrical fire in the attic caused the wiring to short, triggering the doorbell. The Ritcheys chose to believe that God sent an angel to warn them of the fire. The timing was wonderful. They saw God's loving hand and provision throughout the event.

What a privilege to belong to One who knows all things, provides all things, and permits all things for His glory and our good. We are His treasures, and He loves us with an everlasting love.

By God's grace, very few of their personal possessions were permanently damaged by the attic fire. However, everything in the house needed to be removed and cleaned professionally due to smoke damage. During the next few months, while repairs were made and home renovations were being completed, family friends who were spending the winter months in Florida graciously opened their home to the Ritcheys.

Where are your values placed? Are they on things on earth or on things in heaven? The family heritage we have on earth is a shadow or imperfect picture of the family we will belong to for eternity. What a great family celebration we will have as we are seated around the marriage supper of the Lamb! What rejoicing there will be as we are united with the One who provided salvation for us! The last few verses of Hebrews 12 indicate that created things—yes, even those things such as the family heirlooms in which we put such stock here on this earth—will be destroyed. But our inheritance is a kingdom that cannot be shaken, therefore, "let us be thankful, and so worship God acceptably with reverence and awe, for our 'God is a consuming fire'" (NIV).

PART II

THE CALL TO WEST AFRICA—1889-1907

Many disastrous attempts had been made to take the gospel into West Africa. The steaming, swampy, mosquito-infected coast, with sections of forests with dense undergrowth discouraged most explorers. Heat and disease took their toll on early missionaries, leaving graves scattered throughout Liberia and Sierra Leone.

In a series of Bible conferences held by the Young Men's Christian Associations (YMCA) of Kansas, Nebraska, and Minnesota in 1889, a number of young people were moved by the messages of Dr. H. Gratton Guiness, of London, England, as he spoke of the plight of the unreached in the great Soudan. "Year after year, age after age, they fall and perish as though of no more worth than the withered leaves of autumn! They have perished from the earth, and gone into a dark and dreaded eternity, without ever hearing of Him who died and rose that man might live." Nine men and women responded to his challenge and began to make preparations to go to West Africa.

The intentions of this small group reached the ears of the newly formed Evangelical Missionary Alliance (precursor to The Christian and Missionary Alliance, formed in 1897). The members of the new mission organization were thrilled to support this effort to evangelize West Africa. The C&MA's founder Dr. A. B. Simpson had long carried a burden for the "Dark Soudan," of which he had written, "Thou shalt yet be called the Land of Light." He continued, "Every day a thousand lost ones die, ninety millions still in darkness lie; let us listen to their pleading cry, as it echoes from that heathen shore." Here was a group ready to answer the cry and The C&MA was happy to be affiliated with the effort.

In mid-1890, the group of eight missionaries joined the one who had gone before to "sight out the land." However, the climate, malaria, and other diseases quickly took their toll on the early members of the Soudan Mission. Within one month of reaching Sierra Leone, three of the members died. Before the end of the first year two more had died. One of the missionaries noted, "It seems that every forward movement means more missionary graves." However, the remaining missionaries persevered, establishing mission stations and developing the work, which was soon joined by more missionaries.

In 1894, Rev. Roy C. Codding, one of the original members of the first group to go out to Sierra Leone, returned to the States with his wife who was gravely ill from malaria. The heat and disease of West Africa had robbed Mrs. Codding of her strength and she was unable to recover. After her death, as he prepared to return to the field, Mr. Codding wrote a letter to *The Christian Alliance and Missionary Weekly* magazine:

> "Nine of us went there four and a half years ago, and we buried five of our number within the first year. Since then we have buried three more [new missionaries] on the field and my dear wife in this country from the effects of this deadly miasma [malaria]. I praise God for the way He led me to choose that field. He put the foreign work upon my heart; then led me to choose the Soudan because of its unparalleled need and dangers. I had little expectation of living out the first year. Why I did, when five of my companions fell, God alone knows. It seems to me that theirs is the more blessed part—to depart and be with Christ; but while He has work for me I want to be patient and labor on. My dear friends, if God offers you a hard place, get right into it. There is nothing on earth that can give as rich and deep a joy as fellowship with Christ in His sufferings."

Rev. Hal Smith, another missionary wrote at the end of 1904, "It is true we have lost 28 missionaries by death since taking up the work 14 years ago; but what of that? Would any of the great world powers cease to fight even if they lost 28 per minute, as long as there was any vestige of hope for a final victory? Do you realize that 15,000 souls go down to a Christless grave daily in Africa alone? Can you look up in the Master's face and say, 'I am a good soldier of Jesus Christ,' when you allow 28 deaths in 14 years to dishearten you?" Rev. Smith died the following year.

In the years that followed, many others followed in the footsteps of these early pioneers, some of them laying down their lives after a brief missionary career. At one point it was observed that there were more missionary graves than living missionaries in West Africa. The tangible and visible results of more than a dozen years of labors and sacrifice were very limited. West Africa began to be called the land of the "White Man's Graveyard." The Alliance constituency became disheartened and called the effort "The Forlorn Hope." Dr. Simpson offered the missionaries an opportunity to withdraw, but the remaining missionaries resolutely refused, declaring that the land of the "White Man's Graveyard" would one day be known as the land of the "Black Man's Resurrection." They often turned their eyes toward the vast untouched interior of the French Soudan and yearned for the day they could establish a string of mission lighthouses across that dark land.

But in 1907, the tide turned. The Christian and Missionary Alliance magazine noted that at the Missionary Training Institute at Nyack "a mighty spirit of prevailing prayer seized on the group known as the Africa Band; and one after another stepped forward volunteering to go to the front and take the place of those who had fallen. Truly a better day has dawned for the Soudan Mission." As this new wave of missionaries went to West Africa, they came sharing Dr. Simpson's dream to reach all of the Soudan for Christ.

THE BLACK PROPHET—1912-1915

(Note: The details of this story vary from telling to telling. The story recounted here is as it was told to the writer, and as researched from various sources.)

There was an unusual event that took place in West Africa that had nothing to do with any organized mission or decision of a government—it was all the doing of God. About 1912-1913, a 65-year-old black man from Liberia by the name of William Wade *(wah'-day)* Harris was impressed upon by God to go to the neighboring country of Ivory Coast and preach the gospel. As a boy he had attended a British Methodist school. In obedience to God's calling, Harris traveled many hundreds of miles by foot, following the ragged coast lines, traversing bodies of water, and crossing a range of mountains until he reached the area in Ivory Coast known as Jacquesville, which is a tourist attraction today.

The people to whom Harris came were animists; some were even headhunters. Yet, Harris went fearlessly into this land because God had sent him. Wearing the long white robes of a prophet, with a turban on his head wrapped with a red band representing the blood of Christ, he became known as "Prophet Harris." Across his white tunic he wore a red band in the form of a cross. In his hand he carried a bamboo cross—a symbol of the way of salvation through the crucified Christ.

Through interpreters Prophet Harris began to preach in his pidgin English. Within three short years God used him to win well over 100,000 people to Christ. This would be a remarkable feat for any mission or organization to have happen within 20 or 30 years, much less three! The power of God was upon him.

Harris was reminiscent of an Old Testament prophet. With a Bible and a cross, held in upraised hands, he would thunderously command the people to burn their fetishes and turn to the living God who could save them. He preached that the God who created them had sent His Son to earth to die for the sins of men. Harris warned people to turn from their fetishes and never again to return to them lest the wrath of God fall upon them. He carried an English King James Version of the Bible in his hand, and around his wrist he had tied a gourd filled with water with which, in good Methodist fashion he would baptize believers. On occasion, while the converts were burning their fetishes he would break across his knee the bamboo cross he carried and throw it into the flames to show that it was not a new fetish but only a symbol of the cross upon which Christ died for the sins of the world.

As it was in the early church, "And great fear came upon all the church, and upon as many as heard these things." (Acts 5:11). People came from miles around to hear this black prophet. Churches began to spring up through the jungle. This movement remained within 50 miles of the coast, never reaching into the interior.

But the French, hearing of the great religious movement, came with their armies and arrested Harris, in part due to the pressures put upon them by the Catholic church. Also, it was wartime, with The Great War (WWI) in full swing. Any great following of an unknown leader held potential danger to the French colony. There followed a great uprising among his followers who demanded that Harris be released. Fearing the loss of lives the French went to Harris in prison and told him that he would be released in Liberia, but he must agree never again to return to the Ivory Coast. Prophet Harris agreed—with the condition that he be able to address the people one last time. The French agreed.

The message Prophet Harris left with the believers was this: "My people, you have believed the Word of God, which has saved you. You have burned your fetishes—don't turn back to them. Go rebuild the churches the French have destroyed. Buy Bibles from the traders traveling up and down the coast. Put a table in the middle of the church and place the Bible upon it. Go home and wait patiently. Someday a white man with the Book will come to teach you more perfectly the Word of God." For many years after this, the Catholics in the Ivory Coast were known as "the man with the beard" while Protestants were known as "the man with the Book."

Prophet Harris was banished from the Ivory Coast about 1915. Ironically, just a few years later, a treaty would be signed permitting Protestant missionaries into the French colonies. Because of the condition given in the treaty that the gospel could be preached only in the language of the people, many of the English Bibles left by Harris were confiscated and destroyed by the French. But still the people waited for the man with the Book.

THE DOORS OPEN—1917-1930

In 1917, two years after Prophet Harris was expelled from the Ivory Coast, the dream of taking the gospel into the French Soudan was finally within reach of The Christian and Missionary Alliance. While on ship returning to Africa from furlough, Sierra Leone missionaries Rev. and Mrs. A. E. Loose befriended a French official. They questioned him about the possibility of entering French territory to preach, and he assured them he would do all in his power to set up an interview with the French Governor in Conakry, Guinea. Up until this time the French territories had been closed to any Protestant missions. The French colonies were a Catholic stronghold, but more than that, the French were suspicious of any movement that might upset their system of government. All this was about to change.

World War I lasted from 1914-1919. During this time, God was working behind the scenes, using the circumstances and results of the war to open the door for the gospel to be preached in the formerly closed territories of French West Africa. A political redistribution of territory defined the parameters of the French colonies, which began to open in an unprecedented manner to the English-speaking powers. This was because a favorable relationship had developed between France and her allies during the war. Also, treaties of war guaranteed open doors for evangelism as well as for social reform. All of these factors came about to set the stage so that the timing of the meeting with the French Governor was perfect.

Upon reaching Guinea the official kept his word and wrote to Mr. Loose in Sierra Leone to invite him to an interview with the Governor. Mr. R. S. Roseberry accompanied Mr. Loose on this historic occasion. After a favorable interview, the two men took a brief train tour of Guinea and then returned by foot to Sierra Leone because their funds were getting low.

On April 23, 1918, the Governor granted full permission for the missionaries to open Protestant missions anywhere in French territory. The Alliance constituency in the States was elated when they heard the news. In 1919, thirty years after the first small band of missionaries had reached Sierra Leone, the dream of being able to enter the Dark Soudan with the gospel of Christ was to be realized.

From Sierra Leone missionaries moved into Guinea, first establishing a base in Baro. In 1921, at the field conference in Sierra Leone, it was suggested that a number of the Sierra Leone missionaries be transferred to this great new territory to join the three already at Baro.

A map of West Africa lay upon the table, and one missionary dramatically showed the need by placing his thumb on the area representing the work in Sierra Leone. His open hand could not cover the remaining portion of West Africa. After that conference it was determined that a station headquarters would be established at Kankan, Guinea. (Many years later it was moved to Conakry.) From that point on the movement into French West Africa accelerated, with a new wave of missionaries exploring and settling in portions of Guinea, Upper Volta, and Mali.

It was during this time, about ten years after Prophet Harris had been deported from the Ivory Coast, that C&MA missionaries in Guinea, Upper Volta, and Mali began to hear stories of a black prophet who had preached the gospel in Ivory Coast, and about a people who were waiting for the man with the Book.

In 1925, intrigued by these stories, Rev. R. S. Roseberry went on a survey of Ivory Coast accompanied by a few other missionaries. They traveled over dirt bush roads in a Model T Ford until they came into the interior city of Bouake. There they asked if anyone knew of the Prophet or the people looking for the man with the Book. No one had heard of such a thing.

While in Bouake, however, they met a Christian family from Ghana that had moved to Bouake for commercial reasons. When the family heard that the missionaries were in town they came and asked if the missionaries would help to build a church. The missionaries regretfully told them, "You'll have to wait until later. We have a purpose for coming at this time."

For many more days they traveled southward, still trying to locate the people looking for the man with the Book. They had traveled through the dry flat savannas of the north; the rolling partially forested hills of the interior; and now entered the lush, towering forests of the coast. Here trees soared high overhead and dense undergrowth made travel nearly impossible. Draping vines formed a network overhead while across the forest floor ran narrow paths connecting small sunny clearings where villages had been built. It was on these footpaths that the Prophet Harris had traveled spreading the Word of God. It was on one of these same footpaths, well worn by frequent use over the years, that the missionaries made their first encounter with the Harris movement.

The missionaries had arrived to within 50 miles of the coast when one day, through the jungles, they heard the voice of a boy singing a song with a familiar English hymn tune. They broke into the opening where a boy was working in his field. The boy was startled when he saw the white men and ran off into the trees, shouting something they could not understand. The missionaries along with their interpreters followed behind the boy on the path he had taken.

When they reached the outskirts of the forest village they found a large group of people waiting. The people seemed excited as they gathered around the travelers. They called out to one another, repeating the same words over and over again as they touched the white skin of the missionaries. Finally one of the interpreters exclaimed, "They are saying, 'It's the man with the Book! It's the man with the Book! He's come! He's come!'" The long search was finally over.

The missionaries were taken to a mud building in the center of the village. There, planted on the top of the thatched straw roof was a bamboo cross. Inside was a table with an English Bible lying open upon it. The pages of the Bible were worn by hands trying to absorb something of its message and stained by the tears of the people as they had wept over its pages, "Oh God, send us the man with the Book!"

The missionaries began to teach the people through interpreters until dusk. When darkness came they were ushered into a little hut that had been swept clean with a broom made of a bundle of straw. There they set up camp cots and hung the mosquito netting. They fell asleep for a few hours with their lanterns turned on low. It was still dark when a knock came on the wall. "White man! White man! You've slept long enough. Come and teach us more about the Word of God." The missionaries hurriedly dressed and went out to teach by the light of a lantern until daybreak. Stopping only for meals and a few hours of sleep, they continued to teach. For a number of days they stayed in this forest village, teaching the Word, which was absorbed into the hungry hearts of the people.

This scene was repeated as they came upon village after village in the depths of the forest waiting for the man with the book. As they continued on their tour toward the coast, they came to a place where they found a mission work had recently been begun among the Harris churches. They found out that the year before, representatives of the English Methodist mission had stopped in Liberia and received Prophet Harris's blessing to be his representatives to his converts in Ivory Coast.

Roseberry and those with him were overwhelmed by the need for spiritual instruction among the Harris movement. Harris churches, through neglect of many years, had already begun to fall under false teaching and laxity in morals. The need for Christian workers was urgent. However, although their hearts were touched by the need, they did not feel they could step into another mission's area of labor.

Regretfully, they returned to Guinea. It was not until 1929 that another quick survey was taken, and then in 1930, a decision was made to send a missionary couple into Ivory Coast to establish a C&MA mission work. The missionaries would settle in central Ivory Coast among the largest and most responsive tribe in Ivory Coast—the Baoules.

A PEOPLE PREPARED

The call to the Ivory Coast was strong, and the missionaries who had visited Ivory Coast still heard the call to return and teach God's Word. They decided that they would reach the people of the interior—the Baoule tribe. The Ivory Coast has more than 60 ethnic groups. The Baoules of the central region and the Agnis *(ahn'-yees)* of the coast (among the Harris churches) are of the Akan *(ah-kawn')* group, which is the largest subgroup in Ivory Coast.

The Baoules and the Agnis came from the Akan tribal group of Ghana about the mid-1700s. At that time Osei *(oh-say')* Toutou was the king or paramount chief of the large kingdom of the Ashantis with his center of administration in Koumassi. Traditionally the Akan society is matrilineal, even though dominated by men. The king's brother or his sister's son inherited the leadership and wealth of the kingdom.

Tensions often arose between the leader's family who helped him to acquire his wealth and his sister's sons who might one day inherit it. When Osei Toutou died about 1740, his two nephews Opokou Ware *(wah'-ray)* and Dakon fought over who would be the next leader of the powerful Ashanti tribe. Dakon, thought to be the better of the two men, was killed. Dakon had a sister whose name was Abla Pokou.

After Dakon's death, Opokou Ware tried to win Abla Pokou to his side. If he died, another family would assume the dynasty. But if Abla Pokou stood at his side, her child would have the same rights as his own sister's sons.

But Abla Pokou knew that if she remained, hers and Dakon's followers would be treated as inferiors by the followers of Opokou Ware. They decided to escape rather than face servitude. They stole away into the night, taking the road to the west, which led to the Ivory Coast.

When they came to the large Comoe *(co'-mway)* River, they realized they were trapped. They could not get across. With the Ashantis on their heels, they were in a panic. What were they to do? The Akan people always consulted their witchdoctors on matters of importance. The witchdoctors told them that only the sacrifice of a child would be acceptable to the river gods who would make a way for them to cross the river.

Abla Pokou took her only son Kouakou and threw him into the river. As she did so, she cried out in anguish, "Baoule!" meaning, "A child has died!" At great cost to herself, the escape for her people was won.

It is told that at this point large hippos or elephants rose up out of the water and aligned themselves so the people could cross on their backs. Others say that a large tree fell across the river to form a bridge. When the people had all crossed to safety the "bridge" was swept away or submerged in the waters.

Although Abla Pokou's enemies were more numerous than her followers, they could only stand and watch as their quarry fled. Abla Pokou's followers founded the Baoule kingdom located at Sakassou and the two Agni kingdoms at Indenie and Sanwi. They gradually split up into smaller kingdoms, but retained their separate entities even to the present. Most of the chief's traditional authority has been subdued, first by colonialism, and now by modern law, but their ritual authority remains.

It was to this tribe that the Alliance missionaries first went to in Ivory Coast. When they heard the story of "Baoule," the missionaries realized they had a powerful cultural bridge. They joyfully shared the story of how God, like Abla Pokou, sacrificed His Son to die that we might be saved from the kingdom of our enemy, Satan.

THE BEGINNING OF THE WORK—1930-1938

At the West African field conference in 1930, George and Gladys Powell indicated that they felt God was calling them to pioneer the work in Ivory Coast. After prayerful consideration, the Extension Committee approved the appointment.

When the Powells first arrived in Ivory Coast they experienced some difficulty in finding a place to establish a mission station. They were unable to rent quarters in Seguela *(seh'-gway-la)*, so they moved on to Man and then to Daloa. The French officials were not helpful in finding housing for the missionaries and some areas were not convenient because of a lack of food and other necessary supplies.

From Daloa they wired Kankan to ask that their allowance, already late, be sent and to receive approval to move on to Bouake, situated in the center of the Ivory Coast. They waited and waited, but no word came. Their money began to get low and the food supply they had with them dwindled. Day after day passed and no word came from Kankan. Then they learned that the telegraph wires were down because of the rains. At their most discouraging hour, when their funds were down to twenty-eight cents, a telegram came from Kankan with money and orders to go to Bouake.

At Bouake they again searched for a house in which to live. A French trader kindly offered them a room until they could find suitable housing. After about three months and two more moves, they finally settled into a house with reasonable rent. Mr. Powell began to hold church services in a store near the market place. There was a tremendous and immediate response to the preaching of the Word of God as many destroyed their fetishes and turned to the Lord during that first year.

At the field conference at the beginning of 1931, George and Mable Stadsklev, newly arrived on the field, were appointed to join the Powells in Ivory Coast. Three days after conference the two families started their long journey to Bouake in Mr. Powell's car, hauling a trailer that carried all the road baggage. A Dodge truck carrying all of their personal baggage broke down on the road near the beginning of their journey and all ten of them, four adults and six children, had to pile into one car with the cook sitting on the fender to complete the trip. Four days later, on February 15, 1931, they arrived in Bouake. In March the Stadslev's baby boy died of meningitis contracted on the trip.

Bouake was the seat of the Baoule people with a population of about 20,000. It was in these early days of ministry that the Powells first met Julius Roach, a cobbler by trade. He was from Sierra Leone and had traveled around the coast of West Africa, settling in Bouake. Julius had been reared in a Protestant church but had fallen away from the Lord. He had a problem with alcohol and began to earnestly seek God for an answer. He began to pray that God would send a missionary to Bouake to help him. One day he passed a store where he heard familiar hymns being sung. Interested, he peeked in and saw what he knew was God's answer to his prayers. With George Powell's help, Julius sought God for forgiveness and was delivered from his craving for liquor.

Julius became a real student of the Word of God and was soon preaching in different areas. Later, during World War II, he was installed at Dimbokro where he taught the Word for many years until missionaries returned in 1949.

At about the same time, a postman named Nda Moise became a Christian. From Bouake he would ride to M'Bahiakro on his bike, where he would share the gospel. Soon a nucleus of believers developed there, and Moise left his job as postman to become an evangelist. The Stadsklevs helped to minister at the M'Bahiakro outstation.

Everywhere the gospel was spread, the missionaries were overwhelmed by the response. Drawn by the stories of the Harris churches, George Powell and George Stadsklev made numerous exploratory trips to the Swamni area near Toumodi. They rejoiced in finding churches and people waiting for them to come and teach them. Early each morning, usually before breakfast, a bell would ring to announce a church service. By the dim light of flickering lanterns the people would gather to earnestly pray and joyfully sing. The men would put in long, full days, sometimes lasting until 11:00 at night, teaching and ministering until finally their food was gone and the time came to leave. The hunger of the people for the Word of God was overwhelming. Over and over again the invitation would come to teach God's Word.

In 1932, two single ladies, Ruth Liebmann and Elizabeth (Betty) Kennedy, came to the Ivory Coast to join the missionary staff and were stationed at M'Bahiakro. Betty was engaged to marry a young man who was in France for language study. Walter Olsen and Betty planned to be married when Walter finished his study and together they would serve the Lord in the Ivory Coast. Suitable housing was found for the young ladies who would be teachers of the Bible at M'Bahiakro.

That year Mr. Powell was engaged in teaching in a layman's Bible school in Bouake. That same year the Stadsklevs started the station at Toumodi, continuing to reach into the edges of the Harris movement. The field now had three stations in Bouake, Toumodi, and M'Bahiakro.

At Toumodi the Stadsklevs met a young black man who was to play an important role in the furthering of the gospel in Ivory Coast in the years to come. His name was Felix *(fay'-leeks)* Houphouet-Boigny *(oo'-fway boo-ahn'-yee)*. His father was a powerful chief who owned many slaves. He was also a fetisher and worshiped and made blood sacrifices to idols. As a

190

child of privilege, Felix had attended a Catholic primary school, and at the age of 11 had been baptized into the Catholic church. At that time he made a vow that he would never again shed innocent blood as his fathers had done in the past. He asked God to forgive his fathers for the shedding of blood.

Felix continued his education, going on to eventually graduate with a medical degree from the Dakar Medical School. He returned to the Ivory Coast and served as a medical doctor from 1925 to 1940. Houphouet-Boigny loved people and wanted to help them. While he practiced medicine in Toumodi, he also became involved in the political problems of the time. Houphouet-Boigny was also a wealthy planter and understood the problems of the African property owner.

Dr. Houphouet-Boigny attended to the medical needs of the Stadsklevs and their children on numerous occasions. One time, when one of the Stadsklev children became sick from a mysterious illness, Dr. Houphouet-Boigny cared for the child, but refused to tell them what the problem had been until the child recovered. Then he told them that the child had been poisoned. He warned the missionary family about accepting food offered to them by the Ivoirians because animosity against the whites—the French—was strong, and the Baoules were experts in the art of poisoning.

One of the reasons for the animosity against whites was that most of the nationals in the French colonies were drafted to work on plantations, in mines, or on other French projects as part of an imposed system of forced labor under which each male adult was required to work ten days a year to pay his taxes. This system was greatly misused. There was insufficient workforce in Ivory Coast to meet the demand of French plantations and forestry. As a result, a portion of Upper Volta was annexed to Ivory Coast from 1932 until 1947, in order to supply a greater workforce. The African planters, including Houphouet-Boigny, suffered since they were unable to hire an adequate number of workers to work in their own fields. The injustices of the colonial system were a heavy burden for the Ivoirians. Houphouet-Boigny shared the burdens of his fellow citizens and in 1944, he entered the political scene by creating the first African Agricultural Trade Union to fight against injustices.

Before World War II began, Mr. Stadsklev had an experience in the Toumodi area that was to deeply affect him for the rest of his life. He was invited to one of the villages where people were waiting to hear from the man with the Book. When he arrived at the village he was escorted to the home of an elderly man who spoke of how they had been told to burn their fetishes and build a house of God, and that one day, a white man would come to tell the villagers more of God's Word. Twenty years they had waited. As the rainy seasons came and went, their church buildings would degrade and have to be replaced.

The present mud church building was their fifth.

Touched by the thought of all those years passing without a teacher, Mr. Stadsklev taught the Word day after day until it came time to leave. He was asked, "Have you told us all of the stories from the Bible?"

Regretfully he said, "No, but I have to leave or my wife will notify the French commander of my disappearance, and men will be sent to find me."

The old man asked Mr. Stadsklev to accompany him to the village cemetery. There he pointed to all the graves and emotionally accused, "Where have you been these many years? So many waited. So many died. Where have you been?"

The question reverberated in Mr. Stadsklev's mind as he left that small forest village. Upon his arrival at home, he silently brushed past his waiting wife, went in to the dining room where he sat down at the table, laid his head on his arms, and began to sob. His bewildered wife heard him repeat over and over, "Where have you been? Where have you been?"

THE BARRICADES OF WAR—1938-1943

By 1938 the clouds of war were gathering. The missionary staff was small in Ivory Coast. Walter and Florence Arnold were in Bouake with Miss Ruth Liebmann and Mrs. Bell. The Walter Olsens were at M'Bahiakro, and the George Stadsklevs were in Toumodi. The George Powells were on furlough.

In October of that year the boundaries for ministry were established between the C&MA work and the Wesleyan mission work in the Dimbokro area. In addition to this, Mr. R. S. Roseberry had discovered on a tour of the Ivory Coast that the Worldwide Evangelization Crusade (WEC) was taking over a large area of ministry outside the Baoule work in lower Ivory Coast. The burden of reaching the Ivory Coast for Christ was at long last being felt and shared by other mission organizations besides the C&MA, the English Methodist's, and the Mission Biblique of Paris, which had entered Ivory Coast in 1927.

The following year, in 1939, in answer to the earnest prayers of a shop clerk named Joseph Armoh, the Arnolds went to Dimbokro, rented a vacant store, and began a work amongst the Agni. Mr. Armoh had recently come from Ghana and each month when the Stadsklevs came from Toumodi to Dimbokro to do their grocery shopping they would visit with him. He shared with them his concern that there was no missionary work in Dimbokro. He had been praying that a missionary would come and that a school would be started. God answered Joseph Armoh's prayers when He sent the Arnolds to Dimbokro.

From the beginning there was opposition to the gospel being preached in Dimbokro. A local witch-doctor declared, "There will never be a follower of Jesus Christ in Dimbokro!" The Arnolds faced persecution. Their food was poisoned, some of their supplies were stolen, and the efforts to build a church were hindered. But the Christians began to earnestly pray and the attacks ended. The first mud church was completed and the work in Dimbokro was begun.

Walter Arnold had to travel thousands of miles on foot or by bicycle to itinerate because there were no roads in the area. The work was promising, but they were only able to work there for two years before they had to evacuate the Ivory Coast due to the war. In their absence Julius Roach, the Christian layman from Bouake carried on the work in Dimbokro until finally, after the war, Ivory Coast C&MA missionary personnel had increased enough to send a missionary couple back to the area in 1949.

The Olsens, stationed at M'Bahiakro, were to discover another area of ministry as they sent out Jacques, a young native worker, into his home territory of Bocanda with the story of salvation. This was in September of 1939. He was gone so long that they began to worry about his safety. Another worker, Noe *(no'-ay)*, was sent after him and when they finally returned it was with the news that over 200 people had come to the Lord and prayed for forgiveness. The Arnolds were visiting with the Olsens at that time as they were working together on a translation project; they were astounded by the report.

They applied to the French Administration for permission to travel to Bocanda to see if the story was true. At the time, all car owners were ordered to keep their gas tanks filled, ready for their cars to be appropriated by the authorities so they could warn the surrounding area of the encroaching war. The Administrator replied, "If the war starts we will need your car right away to inform the people in the area that we are at war. If you must go, go quickly, but come back immediately!" The next day Walter Olsen and Walter Arnold drove to the Bocanda district and discovered that in one village alone there were 118 new converts! They had to walk for two hours through the dense forest to reach another village where people responded to the invitation to receive Christ that very night. It would not be until after the war, in 1949, that Bocanda would have a full-time missionary working in the district.

In 1940, France fell to Germany and war came to the doors of French West Africa. Communications and supplies were hampered by the restrictions of war. In 1941, French West Africa was cut off from the outside world by a strict blockade. Travel was severely limited. Lack of gasoline restricted the range of missionary travel, and many areas were of necessity unreachable by the missionary.

In spite of the war God was at work in Ivory Coast. In 1941, Itcho *(each'-oh)*, a Djimini *(ji'-mini)* woman from the Katiola *(ka-chee-oh'-la)* area came to George Powell in Bouake and asked for him to "give her the road." She had responded to the challenge to reach her own people for Christ and was returning home. Three weeks later she returned. She reported, "I went to my people and they said, 'We wondered if anyone would come and tell us how we can get to heaven. And now you have come.'" She preached in two towns with many praying in repentance for sins. When she had shared all she knew, the new converts asked her to go back to Bouake and bring a missionary to tell them more.

Marcel Kouassi, a young catechist, was sent to the Djimini tribe and came back with a confirmation of Itcho's report. George Powell was privileged to go to this tribe and share in the discipling of many new converts. He was filled with joy as he baptized them and served communion to his new brothers and sisters for the first time. Marcel Kouassi remained with this tribe for some time teaching and ministering to them. It was a deep shock to the missionaries when Marcel slipped in to the Sunday morning service in Bouake one day to whisper his message to George Powell who was preaching. With tears streaming down his face, Marcel informed him that Itcho was dead, presumed to have been poisoned. Koffi Dan, another lay worker, married Itcho's daughter and together, under continuing persecution from the pagans and Catholics alike, continued the work in the Djimini tribe. Later this area would come under the care of the Conservative Baptists. There are many churches and committed Christians in this area where Itcho first planted the seeds of the gospel.

Wartime conditions in the Ivory Coast were worsening. Most of the missionaries returned to the States, some under extreme conditions. In fact, the ship on which Mrs. Bell (a widowed missionary from West Africa who had come to Ivory Coast in 1938), was travelling with her two children was torpedoed. They were on an overcrowded life raft with others for two weeks before they were rescued. They finally arrived in the States after a great many detours.

In spite of the difficulties of war, visible progress was made on the field as the first church school and the new mission buildings went up on the new mission property in Bouake.

In 1942, George Stasklev left his family in the States and returned to Ivory Coast, travelling 21 days by foot through Liberia to the Guinea border with R. S. Roseberry. From there the two men parted ways, and Mr. Stadsklev found a "charcoal burner" truck (so called because the vehicle was fueled by burning charcoal) to take him to Bouake. He lived in Toumodi for the next two and a half years, with only Paul

Yoma to assist him in the ministry. They walked to the villages, and when his two pairs of shoes wore out he used native-made shoes. Food was scarce, and as a result George's health declined.

The quality of life among the missionaries in West Africa gradually deteriorated. They were literally cut off from the rest of the world. Mail service halted. They became more and more dependent on what they could provide for themselves. Dried bananas were used for sweetening. Rationing was severely limited. There was little to no fuel available, and even the number of candles to burn per month was limited. Inter-mission relationships were strengthened as missionaries came to the aid of and came to rely upon the fellowship of one another.

At a time when the spirits of the remaining missionaries were at the lowest ebb, Mr. Georges Mabille, a French missionary to South Africa, was sent from France to encourage the work. Mr. Mabille had been drafted in 1939 and had to immediately leave his field of ministry to fight for France. In 1940 he was taken prisoner and interned in a prison camp. In September 1941 he was liberated and reunited with his small family, which had made its way with great difficulty to France. In 1941, Mr. Mabille was sent to French West Africa. Mr. Walter Olsen accompanied him on much of Mr. Mabille's tour through the Ivory Coast. Together they witnessed first hand that God was still at work throughout the districts.

In 1942, Mr. Stadsklev was driving through the

bush near Toumodi when he heard a cry for help. Stopping the car and backing up, he was able to look down the embankment and see a car overturned off the side of the road. Trapped inside the car were Dr. Houphouet-Boigny and his chauffeur, a nephew. Mr. Stadsklev helped the dazed, injured men from the car and rushed them to the hospital in Toumodi where they were treated. Dr. Felix Houphouet-Boigny, who later became president of the Ivory Coast, never forgot that a Christian missionary had helped him in a time of need. In September of 1943, Mr. Stadsklev returned to the States in very poor health and was unable to return to the field.

The harsh and racially prejudiced Vichy regime remained in control in French West Africa until 1943, when General DeGaulle assumed control. Finally, by the beginning of 1944, the blockade to French West Africa was lifted and missionaries began to return to the field.

POST WAR DEVELOPMENTS—1944-1990s

The post-war years were a time of change—not only economically and socially, but also in the receptivity of the gospel. It was noted that there was a change in the thinking of the people. Where there had once been observed some opposition to the gospel, now there were new opportunities to preach. A chief who had previously had national evangelists beaten now told Walter Arnold, "Africa is changing. We cannot expect to walk always in the sandals of our grandfathers. I will in no way hinder those who choose to walk in this way."

It was a not only a time of change, it was also a time of challenge. One of the priorities of both the church and the mission was the training of preachers for the work. In 1944, the Bouake Bible School, taught in the native language, was opened and began to address this problem. There were times when it took more than four years for a student to complete his course because of the need for his ministry in the field. The demand for workers was great. With independence came the need for training in the national language of French. To meet that need, in 1964, the Yamoussoukro Bible Institute opened and later in 1993 the West African Alliance Seminary opened in Abidjan.

In 1951, the Baoule national church held its first conference in Bouake. The next year they met again and made plans to move toward self-government. From then they began to further organize and in 1955 moved toward self-government based on self-support. As the national church took over more and more of its own finances, the mission subsidies were greatly reduced; these were healthy signs for the future of the infant church.

The first Baoule New Testament was produced in 1954, the result of many years of labor. (Later, in the 1990s, the Baoule Old Testament was also published.) In 1955, seven national pastors were ordained. New mission stations within the Baoule area were opened from which to preach the gospel.

In 1958, Joseph Koffi, the first ordained pastor of the C&MA in the Ivory Coast, was elected as the first president of the new independent church. It was a joy for the missionaries to set their "child" free from parental care and watch proudly its first tottering steps of independence. The church began to take on more and more of the work in Ivory Coast, leaving the missionaries free to work in developing other areas of ministry.

On the political scene things were changing as well. In 1945, Houphouet-Boigny was elected as one of the two delegates from Ivory Coast to the French Constituent Assembly to meet in Paris. From there he went on to found the Ivory Coast Democratic Party in 1947, and in 1956, he entered the French

Parliament and became the Representative Minister to the President of the Council of France. In 1959 Felix Houphouet-Boigny resigned from the French government to form the first government of Ivory Coast and to lead the country to independence as its first Prime Minister.

On August 7, 1960, Ivory Coast gained its independence from France, and in November, Felix Houphouet-Boigny was elected as the first President of the Republic of Ivory Coast. Felix Houphouet-Boigny was well-loved by the people and was respected by all of Africa who affectionately called him "The Old Man of Africa."

Houphouet-Boigny had a heart that was tender toward God and the things of God. Throughout the years he personally sponsored many religious activities. He rented large stadiums for evangelistic campaigns and provided financial aid and room and board for Christian youth camps. When the Evangelical Federation of Ivory Coast decided to build an intermission Bible college Houphouet-Boigny provided some of his own personal money and property in Yamoussoukro for this project. He would often drive past the building project to see what progress was being made. He provided building supplies and equipment, as they were needed for completing the school and the large C&MA church. In the latter years of his life he built the largest Catholic church in the world in his hometown of Yamoussoukro, Our Lady of Peace Basilica. In his lifetime, he also had built three large religious monuments, a Catholic cathedral, a Muslim mosque, and a Protestant church, in the economic capital of Abidjan as a witness to the world that the Ivoirians believe in God. He was once heard to say, "It is impossible to build a nation unless that nation is built on faith in God."

In 1972 a spiritual awakening began in Ivory Coast beginning with the Neill Foster revival services. It was a historic moment as the missionaries and African workers joined together for a spiritual retreat. In his annual report, field director Fred Polding noted, "Many commented that a spirit of cooperation and love prevailed in the meetings and continues to grow in such a way as we have never known before in the history of mission/church relations. Confessions and reconciliations were made that will transform lives and entire areas of ministry. Profound individual reviving took place which we pray will become a mighty sweeping flame of revival spreading through the entire country."

There followed an air of expectation that culminated the next year when a French evangelist named Jacques Giraud *(jer-oh')* came to Ivory Coast. What followed was known as the greatest religious event in Ivory Coast, since the introduction of Christianity by William Wade Harris. As Jacques Giraud preached the lame walked, the blind saw, the deaf heard, the mute spoke, demons were cast out in Jesus' name, and thousands of decision cards were filled out by individuals wanting to receive Christ. All of the churches and missions in the Ivory Coast benefited by the increased numbers of people seeking Christ. This was a great awakening to the population of Ivory Coast as they witnessed the power of God.

A decade later, on December 11-12, 1982, the national church honored the missionaries by celebrating 50 years of The C&MA presence in the Ivory Coast. The national church arranged the entire elaborate affair. Dr. L. L. King, President of The Christian and Missionary Alliance, was decorated by the government at the end of the program, which was attended by the President of the Ivory Coast. The event was televised and broadcast for several days over national television. It was thrilling to the missionaries to sit and hear from the various speakers as they gave glory to God for all that had been accomplished through The C&MA in Ivory Coast. A clear testimony of salvation through Jesus Christ was given in the service, which was heard by the many representatives from other religions that were present. It was a fitting ceremony in which the child honored the parent. The president of the national church addressed President Felix Houphouet-Boigny who was present for the ceremony on the text, "He whom the Son makes free is free indeed." He went on to say, "Mr. President, we thank you for the liberty you have given us and the freedoms we have enjoyed under your leadership, but you'll never know true liberty and true freedom until you know Jesus Christ, for He is the only One who can give that."

Houphouet-Boigny nodded in agreement while listening to a clear presentation of the gospel.

After a long, benevolent reign as "The Old Man of Africa," President Felix Houphouet-Boigny died on December 7, 1993. While he was alive he cleverly manipulated rival ethic groups for his own purposes and the good of the country; but without his direction, his carefully balanced strategies fell soon after his death. However, he left behind a rich legacy that showed his respect of God, and beginning with Houphouet-Boigny's early contacts with the Stadsklevs, one can see how God had been preparing a leader who would permit God's Word to be spread freely in Ivory Coast.

CONFLICT IN IVORY COAST

Shock waves spread throughout West Africa in September 2002, when General Guei *(guy)* was assassinated in Abidjan and rebel factions took over the central city of Bouake in Ivory Coast. The rebellion spread amid a struggle for political power with clashes between rebel factions, Liberian mercenaries, and government troops; mixed in with anti-French and anti-rebel demonstrations.

By October, most of the missionaries in Ivory Coast were evacuated in a highly publicized and televised drama. In February 2003, one of the missionaries who returned to Ivory Coast e-mailed: "Nearly 63,000 C&MA believers have had to flee rebel-held Bouake. Thousands of these hurting, needy people are in Abidjan. Some have seen family members killed and nearly all have lost all their earthly belongings. They need healing, and God's grace to forgive those who have mistreated them."

March 18, 2003, Wes and Cory Nevius reported on the national church's General Assembly in Yamoussoukro:

> "Joyful were the reunions with dear friends and brothers and sisters with whom we have worked in years gone by in Divo (Dee'-vo) and Abidjan and Bouake. It was heartbreaking and

exhausting to hear the traumatic stories of those having fled from Bouake and other cities in the west. Eyes welling up with tears, explanations flowed of those having walked for hours and hours through the bush, deaths along the way, one pastor's grief at losing seven of his churches as the Christians had to flee before the rebels, and the vice president of one of the churches mercilessly killed. All are displaced, empty-handed, jobless, many are separated from loved ones and without their news.

"Pastor and Madame Sendia and Pastor Antoine, Pastor Adama and others . . . continue to live and minister in Bouake to the remaining sheep there. Three hundred eighty three C&MA national churches were obligated to close due to the hundreds of thousands which had to flee the rebel-held areas.

"Churches continue to swell. They mentioned one man in particular, a very big fetisher in the region who came to the church leaders with several heavy bags, laden with fetishes. These had apparently been used to protect him, his family and his village from the rebels and still they came. His conclusion was that they were worthless and he wanted to be rid of them and to give his life to Christ.

"The sad note of the conference was hearing one story after another of devastation and suffering amongst the pastors. Many have lost everything and are living in one room in a relative's home. Their houses have been looted and many of them have walked long kilometers carrying their children in their arms. Raymond was arrested, at one point, . . . and dragged off into the bush to be shot, saved by the pleading intervention of Pastor Antoine. The suffering and sorrow on their faces is palpable, but their courage is glorious. Their stories were at the same time heart-rending and challenging. Again, we felt privileged to be among them."

Later in March, the Livingstons reported:

"Stories of heroic courage and self-sacrifice overwhelmed us on our two recent trips to Yamoussoukro. The IBACY staff have had as many as 42 displaced people living in their homes at any one time. The campus is awash with children whose parents, unable to care for them, have left them there. Pastor Sraka's wife Jeannette greeted the bag of rice we gave her as a direct answer to her morning prayer. They were confident that God would provide a replacement for their empty bag before the day was out and we, unwittingly, had the joy of being part of that.

"The information on symptoms of trauma in children helped Pastor Bohoussou Raymond understand the behavior his three are manifesting after their escape on foot from Bouake and his near assassination . . . . At one point, while trying to get medical help for their critically ill daughter about curfew time, they were mistakenly shot at as fleeing looters. Theirs is just one of countless horror stories.

"Most pastors have fled (one by swimming a river with his family) but a few have elected to stay in Bouake and minister. The pastoral staff in Yamoussoukro has been receiving, caring for, housing and feeding a steady stream of refugees for six months. Christian doctors are providing free medical care on a short term rotating basis while living in our women's center. It is a humbling experience to watch people who have little stretching it to meet the needs of those who have nothing.

"The political situation remains unclear. A process has been set in place to form a transitional government, but it is not happening smoothly. Deadlines come and go with no clarification of the situation. A recent uprising left dozens of civilians dead, with both sides blaming the other. The recent death in the night of the daughter of seminary students, because the curfew impeded getting medical care for her malaria, and the growing lack of some medicines in the country is one of the uneasy facts of life that make us very hesitant to bring [our] girls back at this time, even though our life on a daily basis is very calm."

Although "peace" in the Ivory Coast continued to be elusive, the church continued to function. Retired missionary Rev. David Arnold returned to Ivory Coast in March 2006 to attend the 75th Anniversary of the church. He noted that although there were police and soldiers at checkpoints about every five kilometers, they were never stopped. For the first time, four national families were appointed as missionaries to other ethnic groups. It was a thrill to see the church fulfilling its mission.

Dave concluded: "The celebration truly was a God-honoring event to thank Him for the 75 years of marvelous intervention in the lives of the Ivorian people. This is a church that is now led by many young dynamic pastors and that has a vision to reach beyond its language borders and seek to win people, who still walk in darkness, for Christ. What a tremendous testimony of the grace and love of God!"

The Seminary in Abidjan continued to operate, as well as the Bible school in Yamoussoukro, preparing pastors to carry on the work of the Gospel. A strong church is arising from the destruction of civil war.

It has been a long, glorious adventure of sowing the seeds of the Word of God in fertile ground where the seeds have taken root and have produced a harvest that is now producing fruit of its own. *"By and by the harvest, and the labor ended, We shall come rejoicing, bringing in the sheaves."*

RITCHEY TIMELINE

1927	11/30	Clyde born
1930	1/20	Doris born
1945-46		Clyde in Merchant Marines (for 1 yr. just as war ended)
1951	6/41	Doris & Clyde graduate from Missionary Training Institute
1952	2/28	Doris & Clyde married
1952-55		Doris & Clyde at Ormond Beach (3 yrs.)
1953	4/23	Brenda born in Volusia County Hospital, Daytona Beach, FL
1954	9/24	Mary Kaye born in Volusia County Hospital, Daytona Beach, FL
1955-56 Sept.		France for language study (1 yr.)
1956-57		Bouake station (actually 10 months) language study (1 yr.)
1957-58		M'Bahiakro station (1 yr.)
1957	12/25	Jon was born at Ferkessedougou hospital
1958-59		Back to Bouake station (1 yr.)
1959	6/6	Judy was born at Bouake, delivered by African midwife
1959		(two weeks after Judy was born) moved to Tiebissou (1 yr.)
1959-60		Brenda's first grade at Mamou, Guinea
1960		Ivory Coast independence
1960-61		Furlough in Florida (came end of July 1960 /left June 9, 1961) (1 yr.)
1961	4/27	Grandpa Ritchey died
1961-65 6/9		Returned to field—Tiebissou station (4 yrs.)
1961-62		Brenda third grade, Mary Kaye second grade at Mamou, Guinea
1962		The year ICA opened

1962	11/18	Dan was born at Ferkessedougou hospital
1965-66		Furlough in Florida and Pennsylvania (1 yr.)
1966-68		Tiebissou station (2 yrs.)
1968-70		Houseparents at ICA—children's dorm (2 yrs.)
1970-71		Tiebissou station (1 yr.)
1971		March Grandma Ritchey and Bill Lauffer visit Ivory Coast
1971-72		Furlough at Toccoa Falls, GA (1 yr.)
1972-74		Houseparents at ICA in H.S. girls dorm (2 yrs.)
1974-76		Bouake station/radio ministry began in '74 until retired
1976-77		Furlough at Toccoa Falls, GA (1 yr.)
1977	June	Bought house in Toccoa, GA
1977-80		Bouake station (3 yrs.)
1979	7/19	Jon attacked by hippo while visiting in Africa
1980-81		Furlough in Toccoa, GA (1 yr.)
1981	3/25	Grandpa Hoover died
1981-85		7-15 returned to Bouake station (4 yrs.)
1983	11/11	Grandma Ritchey died
1983	12/17	Mom & Dad come for Christmas, go back with Danny
1985-86		Furlough in Toccoa, GA (1 yr.)
1986-87		Houseparents in H.S. girls dorm (1 yr.)
1987-91		Bouake station (3-1/2 yrs.)
1991	Nov.	Dad honored by I.C. government (chevalier)
1991	Dec.	Mom and Dad come to States
1992		"Retire" after tour obligations are completed (1/2 yr.)
1997	6/4	Grandma Hoover died

The stories, facts and figures, and historical accounts in this book have been taken from stories related to me over the years, letters and district reports, old C&MA newsletters and magazines, and other sources as a testimony to God's faithfulness and goodness.

Joseph Clyde Ritchey (or "Bud" as
he was called at home).

Bud at the age of three.

The Ritchey home on Conemaugh Avenue.

Clyde in the Merchant Marines at the end of WWII. Third row down, fourth from left.

Clyde's parents, Clyde Sr. and Esther, on the front steps of their home.

Doris's parents, Ethel and Harold
Hoover as newly weds.

The Hoover family: (back, left) Dick, Uncle Walter,
Grandma Clara Hoover Booe, Harold, Ethel.
(Front, left: Uncle Charlie, Margaret, Doris.)

The family Doris left behind when she went to college. Dick was already married and out of the home.

Doris's parents, Ethel and Harold Hoover in their home in Daytona Beach, Florida.

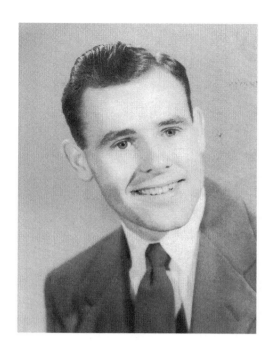

Clyde's college
yearbook photo. 1951.

Doris's college
yearbook photo. 1951.

CONDUCT REVIVAL AT LOCAL CHURCH

Revival meetings are now in progress at the Christian and Missionary Alliance Church at Sta'e

C. Ritchey   **P. Alford**

blvd., under the combined ministries of Paul Alford of Tampa, Fla., and Clyde Ritchey of Portage, Pa. Ritchey is also a talented musician, and both of these young men are graduates of the Missionary Training Institute of Nyack, N. Y.

These meetings will continue nightly at 7:30 through Aug. 19. An unusual degree of interest has accompanied the start of these meetings.

Following graduation from Nyack, Clyde and Paul Alford conducted revival services in various churches in the south.

Clyde's and Doris's engagement photo.

Wedding picture taken in the CBS studios in New York City, New York.

The Ritchey family with Brenda and Mary Kaye, taken at the end of 1954, while in Ormond Beach.

The new church building going up in Ormond Beach.

Late in August a group of twelve new missionaries left for the fields. This was an unusual number to leave at one time. They are pictured on the steps of the New York headquarters following their dedication service. In the front row from left to right are: Margaret Rogers, French West Africa; Virginia Smotherman, Gabon; Mrs. C. W. Good, Peru; Mrs. and Rev. R. C. Griffiths, Colombia. SECOND ROW: *Rev. and Mrs. R. P. Woerner, Chile; Mr. Good.* THIRD ROW: *Rev. and Mrs. D. M. Loose and Mrs. and Rev. J. C. Ritchey, French West Africa.*

Photo of group of new missionaries from the mission magazine. 1955.

Brenda and Mary Kaye with their French babysitter, while Clyde and Doris were in language study in Paris.

Staying in an African home while preaching in a bush village in Ivory Coast. 1956.

Clyde at a baptism.

First Christmas tree in Africa—decorated palm
branches.

The mission house at M'Bahiakro.

The growing Ritchey family with
baby Jonathan Clyde (Jon).

Hunting wild game was a primary source of meat for the
Ritchey table, especially in the early years.

Mary Kaye and Brenda with baby brother Jon.

Jon helping Daddy work on his truck.

Doris with the children on the front steps of the house in Tiebissou. 1959.

Judy with her doll at Tiebissou.

Judy trying to corral her little brother Daniel Dale (Danny).

Clyde cutting Danny's hair.

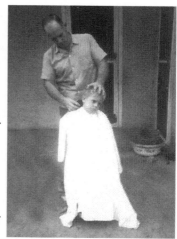

Playing in the sandbox Clyde built for the children while at Tiebissou.

Clyde and Ray Stombaugh with a large capitan Clyde caught.

Presenting a new motorcycle to a young evangelist for his ministry.

Building churches.

Clyde recording a choir.

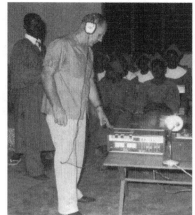

Distributing cassette
players for outreach.

Radio ministry.

The Ritchey family in 1972.

Dorm mother.

Retirement in 1992.

February 2012.

Made in the USA
Charleston, SC
09 July 2014